Sunday
GOD
meets
Monday
MOM

100 Devotions Connecting
Faith and Life

Erin Greneaux

Sunday God Meets Monday Mom
Copyright © 2023 Erin Greneaux

ISBN: 978-1-960292-00-1
E-Book: 978-1-960292-01-8

Scripture quotations marked (NLT) are taken from the Holy Bible, New Living Translation, copyright ©1996, 2004, 2015 by Tyndale House Foundation. Used by permission of Tyndale House Publishers, Carol Stream, Illinois 60188. All rights reserved.

Scripture quotations marked (NIV) are taken from the Holy Bible, New International Version®, NIV®. Copyright © 1973, 1978, 1984, 2011 by Biblica, Inc.™ Used by permission of Zondervan. All rights reserved worldwide. www.zondervan.comThe "NIV" and "New International Version" are trademarks registered in the United States Patent and Trademark Office by Biblica, Inc.™

Scripture quotations marked (ESV) are from the ESV® Bible (The Holy Bible, English Standard Version®), copyright © 2001 by Crossway, a publishing ministry of Good News Publishers. Used by permission. All rights reserved. The ESV text may not be quoted in any publication made available to the public by a Creative Commons license. The ESV may not be translated in whole or in part into any other language.

Scripture quotations marked (TLB) are taken from The Living Bible, copyright © 1971 by Tyndale House Foundation. Used by permission of Tyndale House Publishers, Carol Stream, Illinois 60188. All rights reserved.

Dedication

To my Mother,

Who demonstrated the imperative connection between a flourishing relationship with Jesus and applying faith to daily life in a beautifully imperfect and genuine way. I love you!

Table of Contents

Introduction

To all the moms out there,

I see you. I know you are doing your best, seeking God's guidance, and trying to set a good example. Raising humans is an enormous responsibility, and sometimes the sayings on Sunday seem to fall short when Monday comes along.

But you know what? Believe it or not, the same God who worked miracles in the Bible wants to spend a little time with you today. He is offering you the strength and peace to make it through the challenges you face. Yes, even when the youngest dumps the family size container of goldfish on the floor and dances on them until they are powder.

I have learned in the trenches of motherhood that the real lessons of faith aren't gleaned on Sundays. The true nuggets of wisdom, where the words of the Bible come to life, happen in the chaos of daily interruptions.

For the next one-hundred days, we will laugh and learn together from stories that are too relatable to be fiction. Side by side, we will find peace and encouragement in the truth God speaks for even the smallest moments of life.

Fellow mom, you are not in this alone, even though it feels that way on many days. The God we know on Sunday meets us in the middle of the messiest and most monotonous Mondays. His presence and promises are as relevant today as ever.

Not only is God with you, but so am I and every other mom who has picked up this book. We are all figuring out how to follow Christ and lead our children together.

If you want some accountability and community as you take this journey, I send out a new devotion every Tuesday morning to help us stay encouraged and challenged together.

Visit **https://eringreneaux.substack.com** or use the QR code below to sign up.

I'm cheering for you!

Erin Greneaux

Scan the QR code to sign up for free weekly devotions from the author! These five-minute truths will reset your perspective and help you understand and apply God's Word.

Day One

The Highest Tree

At three years old, Maya is very busy. She doesn't slow down for much, and getting her to stop and sleep is a daily challenge. Yesterday, after leaving a store with my two girls, I told Maya to stand and wait in the grass next to the car while I clipped one-year-old Everly into her car seat. When I turned around to get Maya, she was up in a tree!

"Look, Mommy!" she beamed with pride. "I climbed the highest tree that I could find!"

It wasn't a very big tree, and she hadn't climbed very high, but she had taken advantage of a spare moment to begin a new adventure. In moments like these, I wonder if other parents have toddlers who climb trees while waiting to get in the car or if it's just me.

Read

Be very careful, then, how you live—not as unwise but as wise, making the most of every opportunity, because the days are evil. Therefore, do not be foolish, but understand what the Lord's will is.

Ephesians 5:15-17, NIV

Apply

Each season of parenting brings its unique challenges and reliefs. Whether kids are in school or home full-time, there are still little pockets of time here and there throughout the day. What will we do with those moments? How will we fill them?

Many times, my first reaction is to escape in the easiest way I know how. I pull out my phone, scroll through social media, watch a funny video, or catch up on the half-finished episode of whatever I am currently watching on Netflix. I turn to these things almost like comfort food. The problem is, I never leave those moments with anything of value. They come and go so quickly, and I have squandered them and am left feeling unfulfilled.

Today, let's make the most of every opportunity we have at a spare moment. Instead of scrolling, let's pull out our Bible and invest in our relationship with Christ. Send an encouraging text to a friend that is having a tough day. Serve a neighbor or family member in a thoughtful way. Pray for God's peace in a stressful situation.

Let's look back on our week, knowing that we climbed the highest tree we could find. It may not be very big, and we may not get very high, but we can climb it. Who knows? Our perspective from off the ground may be all that we need to understand what the Lord's will is.

Pray

Father, help me make the most of the time that you give me this week. Show me who I can love or how I can grow in the fleeting moments, so I make the most of every opportunity to bring you glory.

Reflect

What can I do in the spare moments this week that will help me focus on the Kingdom of God?

Day Two

Tucking in Puppy

At age three, Maya is more than a little controlling. She has specific ideas about how everything in her environment should be all the time. She came out of her room after bedtime because she thought she had put Puppy on the sofa to sleep for the night, but to her dismay, she discovered Puppy on the shelf with the rest of the stuffed animals.

She stood in the doorway and began frantically delivering a list of instructions. "Mommy, can you please take Puppy and put her to sleep on the sofa for the night? Tuck her in cozy with the blanket in her favorite spot. Make sure you sing to her and give her a big hug. I'm going to leave her right here by my door for you."

I agreed. She laid the stuffed dog on the floor and reluctantly returned to bed. Sixty seconds passed before the door opened again, this time with Maya holding a blanket. "Mom, I found Puppy's favorite blanket! She can't sleep without it. Please use this blanket to tuck her in. Puppy is still right here. You haven't tucked her in yet. Please don't forget."

I assured her I could handle it, and she went back to bed again. In her world, the stuffed animal is of the utmost importance. Meanwhile, as her mother, I know it is inconsequential in the grand scheme of life. Even so, I place Puppy on the sofa with the blanket and tuck her in carefully before turning my attention to more pressing matters, like paying bills. I do this because, as ridiculous as the request is, I love Maya, and I care about the things that worry her.

Read

Answer me when I call to you, my righteous God. Give me relief from my distress; have mercy on me and hear my prayer. Know that the LORD has set apart his faithful servant for himself; the LORD hears when I call to him. In peace I will lie down and sleep, for you alone, LORD, make me dwell in safety.

Psalm 4: 1, 3, 8, NIV

Apply

We approach God with the same persistent desire to control. We have very specific ideas about how life should go, how we would like for Him to handle certain situations, and how He should care for us. When God is silent about something we think is important or when He doesn't give the answer in our timing, we believe He doesn't care about the issue as much as we do. In actuality, He probably doesn't, but only because He sees the bigger picture.

God hears every request we make, no matter how small or inconsequential in the grand scheme of eternity. No matter how ridiculous the request, He cares deeply for us! No matter what is bothering us, He wants to know about it, and He wants to give us peace so that our worries no longer have a hold over our hearts and minds.

Pray

Father, thank you for caring about the things that worry me, no matter how big or small they are. Thank you for loving me, promising to take care of me, and for being in control of everything so that I can experience rest in your peace.

Reflect

What do I need to pray about today and then release control of?

Day Three

That Looks Familiar

I grew up shopping at second-hand stores and garage sales, and the habit stuck. I love finding an amazing deal, digging through trash to discover a treasure, and experiencing the thrill of the hunt. Going into a store with a rack of the same shirt in multiple colors and organized by size is devastatingly boring.

The other day I was shopping at one of my favorite resale shops that benefits a non-profit for women facing unexpected pregnancy. I love donating to and buying from this little shop. Everly was with me, and I let her pick out a stuffed animal to bring home. She picked out a cat that looked very familiar. While I was sure that Maya had the same one at home, I figured it wouldn't hurt for them to each have their own. When we got home, I told Maya that her sister now had a matching stuffed cat.

Maya looked confused and replied, "But mom, I gave that one away because I didn't want it anymore." It was then that I remembered cleaning it out of her closet a few weeks before and putting it in the bag to donate. We had just bought back the very stuffed animal that we had donated to the store! That's a good business model for them, but not a good shopping strategy for me. It would have been far better for me to have just kept the stuffed animal to begin with!

Read

If indeed they have escaped the corruption of the world through the knowledge of our Lord and Savior Jesus Christ, only to be entangled and overcome by it again, their final condition is worse than it was at first. It would have been better for them not to have known the way of righteousness than to have known it and then to turn away from the holy commandment passed on to them. Of them the proverbs are true: "A dog returns to its vomit," and, "A sow that is washed goes back to her wallowing in the mud."

2 Peter 2:20-22, NIV

Apply

What is familiar to us provides comfort, even if it isn't the best choice. Even though Everly had a hundred new stuffed animals to choose from, she decided on one that was familiar to her. When we entertain certain thought patterns of comparison, dismiss internal issues that need to be addressed, or uphold unrealistic expectations, we reinforce the labels that shackle our identity. We are choosing the same foolishness repeatedly and wondering why nothing ever changes.

Meanwhile, the Bible offers us a store full of new thought patterns, varied choices, and ultimate freedom! However, just like my favorite shopping style, thrifting, it takes a little digging into our souls to uncover the treasure under the clutter of the sinful habits we have collected.

Pray

Father, show me any areas of my heart and mind that continue returning to old habits that you have redeemed. Give me the discernment to recognize those crucial moments of choice and the discipline to choose with wisdom rather than familiarity.

Reflect

What action or thought pattern have I been freed from but continue returning to, anyway?

Day Four

What's in a Name?

My toddler loves to name things: her stuffed animals, dolls, and any creatures she discovers in the wild. She fills a morning trip to the zoo with her insistent need to name every animal we encounter. Her names are not very creative, but they are descriptive.

She names a beautifully feathered parrot "Colorfully." A toy pony with a pink mane is called "Pinky." Her modeling clay, shaped into what is supposed to be a giraffe, she refers to as "Squishy."

These names do not reflect the things' true nature, value, character, or quality; they simply comment on the outer appearance at first glance. The names are merely superficial descriptions.

Read

See what great love the Father has lavished on us, that we should be called children of God! And that is what we are! The reason the world does not know us is that it did not know him.

1 John 3:1, NIV

But to all who did receive him, who believed in his name, he gave the right to become children of God, who were born, not of blood nor of the will of the flesh nor of the will of man, but of God.

John 1:12-13, ESV

Apply

As moms, we often give ourselves names. Maybe we name ourselves "the mom who is always late." Or "the mom who doesn't recognize her body anymore." Sometimes even, "the mom who has no idea what she is doing."

Even though these labels only describe us, too often we allow them to *define* us. This beautiful passage in 1 John reminds us we have only one true name, and it is "Child of God."

It is difficult to remember our true identity because the world judges and labels based on the outward appearance. If people don't know our Father, they will not recognize us as His children. Fortunately, we know the opinion of the only One who matters, our Father.

Even on the days when we don't measure up, feel defeated, and commit every mom fail in the book, those actions do not define our identity. My true name, and your true name, is "Child of God."

And that identity will never change because we did nothing to earn it! He offers it to us freely because of His love and grace. There is no pressure to "be enough" because we come empty-handed, and God calls us His own anyway.

Pray

Father, thank you for your love, which defines who I am and gives me confidence in your power to continue to mold me into Christ-likeness. Help me recognize the false labels that I have given myself and replace those lies with your truth.

Reflect

What name or names have I given myself and allowed to define my identity?

Day Five

Can You Feel the Love?

Maya can read my mind, I know it. Sometimes while I watch her play, I look at her, and my thoughts are far from lovely.

I think, 'How did she get that huge knot in the back of her hair? I wish she would let me brush it out. It amazes me how this girl can go from being groomed to looking homeless so quickly.'

She looks up from her toys, and I can tell by the self-conscious look on her face that she knows what I'm thinking. I immediately regret it.

Thankfully, it works both ways. Sometimes I stare at her in amazement as she colors a picture. I think, 'Look at this beautiful face and those eyes so concentrated on her work. She is such a thoughtful girl, and so smart. Did Nathan and I really make this? I love her so much!'

She looks up from her drawing and with a beaming smile, throws herself into my arms for a giant hug. She knows. My love for her and my thoughts about her reverberate from every unspoken expression of my being, and she knows. Without me even having to ask, Maya gives me the gift of her embrace.

Read

I will exalt you, my God the King; I will praise your name for ever and ever. Every day I will praise you and extol your name for ever and ever. Great is the LORD and most worthy of praise; his greatness no one can fathom. The LORD is gracious and compassionate, slow to anger and rich in love. The LORD is good to all; he has compassion on all he has made. All your works praise you, LORD; your faithful people extol you. They tell of the glory of your kingdom and speak of your might, so that all people may know of your mighty acts and the glorious splendor of your kingdom. Your kingdom is an everlasting kingdom, and your dominion endures through all generations. The LORD is trustworthy in all he promises and faithful in all he does. The LORD upholds all who fall and lifts up all who are bowed down.

Psalm 145:1-3, 8-14, NIV

Apply

We know that God really can hear our thoughts, but we rarely consider that our thoughts matter to Him. In the same way that our children thrive under our loving gaze, God revels in the moments that we show Him our devotion through gratitude and praise. God created us to glorify Him, and when our thoughts and actions declare His glory with shouts of exultation or we sit silently in awe of His majesty, we fulfill our purpose. When we take on a posture of praise, we place God on the throne of our hearts and experience the peace that comes with His preeminence.

Pray

For our prayer time today, let's not ask for anything. Let's simply pray words of adoration to our King from the Psalm above. Linger over the lines and let your entire being reverberate your posture of humble gratitude and praise.

Reflect

In what ways do I experience God's pleasure when I live in an attitude of thanksgiving?

Day Six

No More Yellow

Do your kids have a favorite color? Maya loves every color except yellow. She. Doesn't. Like. Yellow. I have heard of kids not liking a color, but Maya takes her dislike to the extreme.

When we were purging toys a few weeks ago, she separated out all the yellow crayons from her crayon bucket and gave them to me, saying, "You can give these away. I don't like the yellow ones."

Then one day during her nap time (which is really just resting time because this girl does not turn off), I heard a commotion in her room and found all of her books scattered across her bedroom floor. She had carefully separated out every book that had a yellow cover.

Without an explanation, she simply handed me the stack and said, "I don't want these books on my shelf."

I do not know how long it took her to work on that, but she has a dedication to her dislike that I find impressive. In her mind, life without yellow books and crayons is better than life with them, even though it means getting rid of some things.

Read

If your right eye causes you to sin, gouge it out and throw it away. It is better for you to lose one part of your body than for your whole body to be thrown into hell. And if your right hand causes you to sin, cut it off and throw it away. It is better for you to lose one part of your body than for your whole body to depart into hell.

Matthew 5:29-30, NIV

Apply

I always thought that this verse was a little extreme and dramatic, but I think that is the point. Sin is nothing to experiment with. If we allow it to stay in one small area of our lives, it grows and takes over like weeds in a neglected garden.

We must actively seek any trace of it in our lives and intentionally separate it out so that it has no hold on us. Otherwise, it will steal not only the area of our lives that it occupies, but our entire being. We must be thorough in our mission to scrub sin out of every part of our lives that it entangles.

Seeing Maya's determination to rid her world completely of the color yellow has given me a new resolve to search my life for any thoughts that are unhealthy, any words that aren't loving, and any attitudes that are self-serving. I am determined to toss them out like the filth they are. Our lives are more complete when we take certain things away, especially when those things do not align with God's character. It would be a tragedy for us to gain the world but lose our souls.

Pray

Father, show me which sin in my life is going unnoticed and unchecked. Give me the resolve to separate it out, not counting it as loss, but as incredible gain. Thank you for your unending faithfulness to forgive me and restore me.

Reflect

What sin do I need to eradicate from my life? What are some practical steps that I can take to do that this week?

Day Seven

A Lesson Learned

Just one month into Pre-K3, Maya amazes me with all the things that she is learning. I can tell exactly what her teacher says in the classroom because Maya puts it into practice immediately, although not by changing her behavior or applying it to herself. Instead, she implements her newly discovered knowledge as a tactic to control her little sister.

Her constant narrative goes something like this:

"Everly, sit crisscross applesauce."

"Everly, we do not push our friends. Keep your hands to yourself."

"Everly, one, two, three eyes on me. I said, 'EYES ON ME!'"

At eighteen months old, Everly is tired of being groomed into a preschool student. I keep imagining how wonderful it would be if Maya put into practice for herself the simple truths she tries to impose on her sister. While she can identify the ways for her others to improve, she doesn't recognize her own need for change.

Read

Then Jesus said to the crowds and to his disciples: "The teachers of the law and the Pharisees sit in Moses' seat. So you must be careful to do everything they tell you. But do not do what they do, for they do not practice what they preach. They tie up heavy, cumbersome loads and put them on other people's shoulders, but they themselves are not willing to lift a finger to move them."

Matthew 23:1-4, NIV

Apply

I love when Jesus comes down on the Pharisees in the Bible, but my excitement wanes when I discover we might actually be members of the group He is calling out. How often do we read the Bible or hear a message in church and immediately think of a person who we wish were hearing those words? How often do we think, 'If only so-and-so could learn to apply that!'

In taking that stance, we miss out on the beautiful opportunity to grow personally in our relationship with Christ. We trade a moment of revelation and growth for a moment of judgment and silent accusation. What lesson did God have for us in that moment that we missed while being too busy focused on others? What promise did He want to whisper to our hearts? What grace did He desire to extend to meet us in our weakness?

Instead of embracing the gift of being shaped by the of the God of the Universe, we trade humility for pride, a teachable heart for one of arrogance, and an obedient spirit for one of judgment. What a tragedy! We learn the Word, but miss its purpose.

Pray

Father, help me to not only know your Word, but to apply it to my life. Allow me to hear the hard truths that you have for me and be open to learning humbly from them, rather than being quick to hold others accountable to those same truths.

Reflect

What spiritual lesson do I know well enough to hold others accountable to, but need to actually apply in my own life?

Day Eight

Turn It Louder

The only way to make a hot summer day in Louisiana bearable is to splash some water on it. We have a mermaid sprinkler, and my girls love playing in it. When the water pressure is high enough, the mermaid spins around, spraying water in every direction.

Maya is my adventurous girl, and she is constantly telling me to "turn the water louder," which is her way of letting me know we need more water pressure to get the mermaid spinning.

Everly is more reserved in her sprinkler preferences. She likes the water pressure low and predictable. As soon as the mermaid spins and things get chaotic, she backs away.

Read

The thief comes only to steal and kill and destroy. I came that they may have life and have it abundantly. I am the good shepherd. The good shepherd lays down his life for the sheep. I am the good shepherd. I know my own and my own know me.

John 10:10-11, 14, ESV

I have told you these things, so that in me you may have peace. In this world you will have trouble. But take heart! I have overcome the world.

John 16:33, NIV

Apply

John 10 gives us a picture of Jesus as our Shepherd, faithfully leading us as His sheep. Many times we assume that having life to the full means having more of just the good parts of life. In reality, having life to the full simply means having more life. It takes life and turns it "louder." We have higher highs and lower lows.

The picture of Christ as a shepherd is such a powerful one because it addresses all the lows that come into play: wolves attacking the flock, sheep wandering off, and thieves breaking in to steal the sheep. Having the Shepherd doesn't stop these things from happening, but it provides a haven for the sheep amid the turbulence.

He assures us that the safety of the sheep is so important that He lays down His life to protect them. When we sign up as one of Christ's sheep, we agree to follow Him no matter where He leads. Our previously lazy sheep life suddenly looks more adventurous, more full.

There will be days when this full life seems to spin out of control, but we have the assurance that our Shepherd is vigilant and is guiding us well. Instead of backing away in fear, we can confidently step into the unknown, expecting our Shepherd to turn life "louder!"

Pray

Father, help me trust you in the moments that I back away instead of stepping confidently into the adventure of each day. Give me faith to follow you into each high and low, knowing that you gave your life for me.

Reflect

In what areas of life do I ask God to turn things "louder?" In what areas do I back away?

Day Nine

Pretending to Sleep

As soon as Maya moved from her crib to a bed, she began creating reasons to get out of it. She needs a million things at bedtime: a drink of water, a special stuffed animal, a song, a book, one more hug, etc. In the mornings, she is awake bright and early, her face peering into mine at the bedside, whispering, "Mom, is it time to get up yet?"

On occasion, I will be awake in bed before she wakes up, preparing mentally for the day ahead. When I hear her door open and her footsteps pad toward our bedroom, I close my eyes and pretend to be asleep. I lay still, holding my breath, hoping that she will go back to her room for a little more rest. It rarely works, but I try anyway.

Read

Here I am! I stand at the door and knock. If anyone hears my voice and opens the door, I will come in and eat with that person, and they with me.

Revelation 3:20, NIV

But while [the son] was still a long way off, his father saw him and was filled with compassion for him; he ran to his son, threw his arms around him and kissed him.
The son said to him, "Father, I have sinned against heaven and against you. I am no longer worthy to be called your son."
But the father said to his servants, "Quick! Bring the best robe and put it on him. Put a ring on his finger and sandals on his feet.

Bring the fattened calf and kill it. Let's have a feast and celebrate. For this son of mine was dead and is alive again; he was lost and is found." So they began to celebrate.

Luke 15:20b-24, NIV (brackets added for context)

Apply

Many times, we picture God as a parent trying to get a little more rest. When we pray, we may feel like we are bothering Him and that our prayers are being purposefully unheard. If we view God based on our own parenting, we will never understand the true nature of His love because we are imperfect.

However, the Bible gives us a completely different image of God. Instead of pretending to be asleep while we intrude through the door to reach Him, God is the one taking the initiative. He is the one knocking on the door, waiting patiently for us to open it and let Him into our lives. He is the Father, running to embrace us even after we have made every mistake possible.

What a powerful change in perspective! He shows an urgency, a desire to be with us, and an unfailing resilience in His efforts that shatters our misconceptions about His ambivalence. He is the One pursuing us!

Pray

Father, thank you for being a God who pursues me! When I am tempted to believe that you are distant or uncaring, help me remember this demonstration of you standing at the door of my heart and knocking.

Reflect

When was a time in which God seemed distant from me? What happened that helped close the gap?

Day Ten

Weaning

Weaning each of my girls was a bittersweet experience. There is something so beautiful and intimate about the mother-child connection that breastfeeding creates. It is precious, but there is a co-dependence in that season that is unsustainable. Babies need to eat every few hours, disrupting the mom's sleep and any form of productivity.

At some point, the child and the mother need time apart for different activities, and a slow separation encourages an establishment of independence. Not only did I enjoy the increased freedom that came with weaning, but my girls developed a new level of mobility and social interaction with others.

Read

My heart is not proud, Lord, my eyes are not haughty; I do not concern myself with great matters or things too wonderful for me. But I have calmed and quieted myself, I am like a weaned child with its mother; like a weaned child I am content.
Psalm 131:1-2, NIV

For everyone who lives on milk is unskilled in the word of righteousness, since he is a child. But solid food is for the mature, for those who have their powers of discernment trained by constant practice to distinguish good from evil.
Hebrews 5:13-14, ESV

Apply

For a long time, I didn't understand why the calm and quiet child in this verse was the one that was weaned. In my experience, the quickest way to calm a crying baby is to breastfeed. However, once I weaned my girls, it all became clear. A weaned child can rest with its mother, because she isn't demanding anything from her. A weaned child cuddles up with mom for the sake of her company and nothing else. Instead of asking for something, she finds peace in her mother's presence alone.

So many times we go to God looking for something. We want answers to questions, relief from trials, deliverance from temptations, and miraculous results to prayer. None of this is wrong. However, the way to find contentment is simply to be with God for the sake of the intimacy of His presence.

We must lay aside our demands and approach Him as a little child. A child who acknowledges that she is not in control. A child who has already received all that she needs and is now satisfied. A child who completely trusts God to handle all of her cares and worries. This child is humble, surrendered, and at peace.

Do you desire that posture as much as I do? Even while the uncertainty of life is swirling, we can run to God and find rest, as a weaned child does with her mother.

Pray

Father, help me approach you with humility, trusting that you are in control and that I can rest. Give me a desire to spend time with you for your own sake, and not for what you can give me.

Reflect

What stands in the way of my spending time with God solely for the sake of enjoying His presence?

Day Eleven

Grocery Store Snacks

Every time we go to the grocery store, my girls want a snack. How could they not, while in a store completely dedicated to food? Even as we walk in, I know which requests I will say yes and no to. Animal crackers, candy, and cookies are a no because they will end up all over the grocery store floor.

I will say yes to produce that is healthy, within my spending budget, and priced by quantity rather than weight. This means saying no to apples that sell by the pound, but yes to cucumbers that are priced individually, so I can be sure to pay for them.

I know that my yeses and nos must seem random to the girls since they don't know the pricing methods of each type of produce, but I have good reasoning for each of my answers. They are slowly learning which requests I will say yes to.

Read

Ask and it will be given to you; seek and you will find; knock and the door will be opened to you. For everyone who asks receives; the one who seeks finds; and to the one who knocks, the door will be opened. Which of you, if your son asks for bread, will give him a stone? Or if he asks for a fish, will give him a snake? If you, then, though you are evil, know how to give good gifts to your children, how much more will your Father in heaven give good gifts to those who ask him!

Matthew 7:7-11, NIV

Apply

So many times we come to God with a request, knowing that He will answer yes or no, and we feel like His answers are unpredictable and random. Here is what we know from the Bible about His answers:

- They are for our good.

- They will always line up with the laws set forth in His Word.

- They will fall within our "budget" of what He knows we can steward well.

In the same way that my children must trust my reasoning when making decisions, we must trust our Heavenly Father to know what is best for us. We must acknowledge that He can understand and foresee our needs better than we can. When God says yes to our prayer, we can trust that He will equip us for any challenges that it may bring.

When God says no to our prayer, we can rest with patient assurance, knowing that He is looking over all the options and sees a wide variety of choices that are wonderful possibilities. Instead of asking "why not?" let's strive to change our perspective to see which other choices coincide with His will and plans for us.

Pray

Father, when your answer to my prayer is no, help me remember that you have wonderful gifts that you long to share with me. Help shift my perspective, and give me discernment so that I can know which gifts to ask for.

Reflect

What is one prayer God answered no to that I am grateful for in retrospect?

Day Twelve

The Writing on the Chair

Three-year-old Maya was supposed to be in her room for "resting time" since naps are long over. Instead, I found her in the recliner in the den. Behind her was a beautiful drawing, written in pen, covering the fabric chair from top to bottom and side to side.

When she didn't seem to see the issue, she unknowingly nominated herself as my helper in cleaning off the marks. It took the two of us an entire hour of scrubbing and the better part of a bottle of stain remover to clean up what had taken her only a few minutes to apply. However, we were eventually successful in removing all the marks. Not even a trace remained.

Read

But this is how God fulfilled what he had foretold through all the prophets, saying that his Messiah would suffer. Repent, then, and turn to God, so that your sins may be wiped out, that times of refreshing may come from the Lord, and that he may send the Messiah, who has been appointed for you—even Jesus.

Acts 3:18-20, NIV

Then [Jesus] said to them, "My soul is overwhelmed with sorrow to the point of death. Stay here and keep watch with me." Going a little farther, he fell with his face to the ground and prayed, "My Father, if it is possible, may this cup be taken from me. Yet not as I will, but as you will."

Matthew 26:38-39, NIV (brackets added for context)

Apply

We know that through Christ, we experience complete forgiveness from our sins. No matter how many mistakes we have made, they are never more than God can remove. But many times, we mistake the totality of God's forgiveness for effortlessness.

Just because God removes our sins completely doesn't mean that their removal doesn't come at a significant cost. Although Maya and I could indeed make the chair "all better," it took a lot of work to get it that way.

In the same way, God's ability to cast our sins "as far as the east is from the west" came at the price of Jesus' blood shed on the cross for us. This incredible act of love and submission by God's own Son is beyond our comprehension. And yet, in order for the price of our sin to be paid, every bit of His suffering was required.

Before Maya writes on the furniture again, I hope she remembers the hour of scrubbing that it took to remove the last set of marks. And the next time I consider acting in disobedience, I hope I remember the severity of the price Jesus paid on the cross.

Pray

Father, thank you for sacrificing your own Son to pay for the price of my sin. When I ask you for forgiveness, let me never forget the cost of your ability to forgive. Help me experience the full freedom that your forgiveness provides and forgive others as freely as you forgive me.

Reflect

How have I made light of God's forgiveness by mistaking it as something easily accomplished?

Day Thirteen

In Utero

At one year old, my middle daughter, Everly, woke up during the night not feeling well. Every time I tried to put her back to sleep in her crib, she would give the saddest little cry. I ended up laying in the crib with her to calm her down enough to go back to sleep.

She snuggled next to me, sticking her toes between my knees and wrapping her arms around me. Her fingers and toes twitched as she drifted off to sleep, seeming as though my skin was moving and not hers.

The strange sensation brought back vivid memories of feeling her move inside my belly before she was born. She and I were so intimately connected, not only did my movements affect her, but I felt each of hers inside of me. We acted as one body. My routines, food choices, and exercise habits fueled her development. We were inseparable; distinct, but one.

Read

Don't you believe that I am in the Father, and that the Father is in me? The words I say to you I do not speak on my own authority. Rather, it is the Father, living in me, who is doing his work. Believe me when I say that I am in the Father and the Father is in me; or at least believe on the evidence of the works themselves. Very truly I tell you, whoever believes in me will do the works I have been doing, and they will do even greater things than these, because I am going to the Father. And I will do whatever you ask in my name, so that the Father may be glorified in the Son. You may ask me for anything in my name, and I will do it.

John 14:10-13, NIV

Apply

As Christians, we go through seasons in which we may feel closer or more distant from God. Thankfully, those feelings do not reflect the reality of our relationship with God. No matter how much or little we can sense God's movement, we are still intimately connected with Him.

The Holy Spirit is inside of us, nudging us in the direction we should go, felt deep within our being. And we are in Christ, forgiven by the power of His sacrifice on the cross, presented as pure and blameless daughters to God. And Christ is inside the Father, doing the work that He has determined before the foundations of the world.

When so encapsulated in our Heavenly Father, how could we ever doubt His love or our ability to accomplish on His behalf things that we could never do on our own? Even when we can't feel His presence or lose sight of His direction, we are exactly in the center of His hand, just as a baby in the womb need never fear the absence of her mother.

Pray

Father, thank you for the assurance that I will never leave your hand. Thank you for Jesus' sacrifice, which allows me to embrace being your child without condemnation. Show me the good work that you have for me to do and give me your strength to accomplish it.

Reflect

Do I take the time to feel the direction in which the Lord's Spirit is moving me?

Day Fourteen

The Amaryllis

My paternal grandfather is a faithful gardener. He recently gifted me a beautiful amaryllis that had a giant cluster of buds, and I put it in the ground immediately. Within a few days, the buds opened to show off the most gorgeous blooms. As breathtaking as the flowers are, the most impressive part of the plant is underground.

To plant the amaryllis, I took it out of the pot that I received it in and shook the loose dirt away from the bulb. I have never seen a bulb this large in my life. It was eight inches across and had a crown of ten to twelve smaller bulbs around it, a ring of little babies all growing from the energy of this massive ball.

Garden centers don't sell bulbs like this. It grows slowly over years or decades. It is faithfully and carefully tended and nurtured. This plant is such a meaningful gift, and I will enjoy the flowers for years to come. Someone else put in the work to make this plant thrive.

Read

Blessed is the one who does not walk in step with the wicked or stand in the way that sinners take or sit in the company of mockers, but whose delight is in the law of the Lord, and who meditates on his law day and night. That person is like a tree planted by streams of water, which yields its fruit in season and whose leaf does not wither— whatever they do prospers.

Psalm 1:1-3, NIV

Apply

If my grandfather is a faithful gardener, I can apply the term even more fittingly to his walk with the Lord. He is a man who has kept faith through difficulty and blessing, in want and plenty, and in loss and life, and continues to do so at ninety-four. He gave the most meaningful gift: the legacy of a life devoted to Christ that he impressed on my father, that my father impressed on me, and that I am impressing on my own children.

The beautiful flowers that others see as they look at my Pop Pop's life are not by chance. They are rooted in consistent obedience to Christ for almost a century. Living waters feed the bulb-like core of his soul. Just like my amaryllis bulb, his authentic faith has created a crown of believers who have grown because of his life, a colony of plants that will grow long after his stalk of flowers fades.

There is no greater gift that we can leave to our children than the example of a life dedicated to Christ. If you see the flowers of joy, peace, patience, and love displayed in others, they result from a deep relationship with Christ that is unseen. In a culture that increasingly celebrates making every aspect of life a public spectacle, we must make it a priority to grow privately if we want our faith to have a lasting impact for generations.

Pray

Father, thank you for desiring to know me personally. Help me make my time with you a priority. Give me the faithfulness to grow in you until the fruit of the Spirit in my life reflects the life I find in you. Allow me to leave a legacy of intentional devotion for you to my family and friends.

Reflect

How well am I tending to the unseen parts of my life? Am I investing in my private relationship with Christ?

Day Fifteen

Bedtime Lullabies

Every night, I sing a lullaby to Maya. It is the same one that I have sung over her every night since before she was born. I would love to say that these moments at bedtime are a sweet time of connection, my daughter basking in the love of her mother's presence. Far from it.

She fills these moments with last-ditch efforts to get what she wants, interruptions intended to earn a few more minutes of time awake, and wiggling around to expel the final ounce of her pent-up toddler energy. I sing through frustrated sighs while trying to get her feet off of my face and take off her fairy wings. As I wrangle her under the covers, she charges the bed sheets like a bull at a red cape.

I reminisce about the days when she was my sweet little baby, and she snuggled close to my chest as I sang these words. Those moments of beautiful connection were the daily reality for a long time, and I miss them.

Read

The Lord is my shepherd, I lack nothing. He makes me lie down in green pastures, he leads me beside quiet waters, he refreshes my soul. He guides me along the right paths for his name's sake. Even though I walk through the darkest valley, I will fear no evil, for you are with me; your rod and your staff, they comfort me. You prepare a table before me in the presence of my enemies. You anoint my head with oil; my cup overflows. Surely your goodness and love will follow me all the days of my life, and I will dwell in the house of the Lord forever.

Psalm 23, NIV

Apply

As much as I desire to have moments of contented communion with my daughter, I rarely translate that same desire into my relationship with God. When I spend time in prayer, I seldom focus on simply dwelling in His presence and enjoying His company. It is more often a frantic request for aid, a heartfelt prayer for intervention, or a rehashing of the day with a cobbled-together sense of gratitude for the highs and lows. When we approach God this way, I am thankful that God has infinite patience, unlike me with my toddler.

God wants to rescue us in our time of need and hear about the concerns of our day, but more than anything, He desires for us to enjoy His presence. God wants us to present our worries but then settle into a peace, knowing that He is in control and He loves us. He will take care of us. He will not forsake us. If we can stop trying to negotiate for what we want and worrying about what we need, we will realize He is the answer. His presence is more than enough. We can lay our head on His chest, and rest in Him.

Pray

Father, thank you for hearing my prayers and being an active participant in my life. Help me bring my worries and frustrations to you in surrender. Allow me to rest in peace, knowing that you are taking care of me. Give me a desire to abide in your presence.

Reflect

How can I be intentional about spending time simply being in God's presence?

Day Sixteen

Caterpillars in the Garden

The girls and I have a vegetable garden in the backyard. I try not to take it too seriously because the girls regularly uproot plants, sow the seeds in a single clump, and pick vegetables long before they are ripe. It is a garden intended to teach my children how food grows, which puts it at significant risk of being destroyed.

Recently, I discovered some caterpillars on the green bean plants. I showed Maya how to take them off and instructed her to squish them so that they wouldn't eat the plants. She was appalled at my suggestion and launched into a long explanation of how the caterpillar was her pet. He liked to eat green bean plants, and it wouldn't hurt if we let him stay and live there on his favorite food.

I countered by telling her that the caterpillar would eat all of our plants, turn into a butterfly, and then lay a bunch of eggs of new caterpillars that would eat more of our plants. Even though he liked green beans, we like them too, and he wouldn't be considerate enough to leave any for us to eat.

Read

Do not give dogs what is sacred; do not throw your pearls to pigs. If you do, they may trample them under their feet, and turn and tear you to pieces.

Matthew 7:6, NIV

Apply

We often give our best to things that are ultimately worthless. I hate saying it so bluntly, but it is one of our strongest tendencies as humans. We pay the most attention to the opinions that matter the least, we give our time to activities that lack meaning, and we offer our devotion to worthless idols. We see the caterpillars in the garden of our hearts, and instead of squashing them, we think that sharing a little of the produce won't hurt.

God is at work pointing out the places in our lives that have taken what is sacred and handed it over to something worthless. He doesn't do this out of cruelty, but out of love. He wants us to protect our eternal treasures so that we can one day stand before Him and hear the words, "Well done, good and faithful servant" (Matt. 25:23).

God wants the produce of our souls to grow and flourish so that it nourishes our relationship with Him. He wants to guard the sacred places of our lives that are reserved for Him alone. He wants to spare us from the moment of realization that we have spent our best time, energy, and affection on worthless things. He wants us to have the full satisfaction of a life well-lived and wisely invested.

Pray

Father, help me recognize the temporary things in my life that I allow to put the eternal at risk. Give me the initiative to remove every distraction that comes between who I am today and who you desire for me to become.

Reflect

What things in my life are taking away from what is eternal?

Day Seventeen

Go, Go!

As Everly approaches the age of two, her opinions and her ability to make those opinions known are advancing exponentially. A few months ago, she started a new habit. Every time we ride in the car and come to a stop sign or red light, she calls out, "Go, Mommy!"

Even with her car seat facing the rear of the vehicle, she senses the change in motion and feels the need to get things back on track. This week my older daughter fell asleep in her car seat on a family outing to the grocery store. I told my husband to run in for the few necessary items, and I would wait in the car with the girls so that Maya could keep sleeping.

I parked the car, excited at the possibility of a few minutes of silence. However, as soon as Nathan got out, Everly began her usual demand.

"Go, mommy! Mommy, go! Go, go!"

She would not let up. After ten minutes straight, I finally started circling the parking lot just to keep her satisfied, afraid that she would wake up my other daughter. Sure enough, as soon as the car began moving, she happily played in her seat without a word. It didn't matter that we weren't actually heading towards a destination. Constant movement was her chief priority.

Read

But they who wait for the Lord shall renew their strength; they shall mount up with wings like eagles; they shall run and not be weary; they shall walk and not faint.

Isaiah 40:31, ESV

Apply

How often do we fall into the same misconception of stillness as undesirable? We mistakenly believe that movement equals progress. When God asks us to slow down, or heaven forbid, to come to a complete standstill, we beg to get things moving again. And if we stay in one place too long, the feeling of being stuck is so agonizing that we would rather circle pointlessly than stay still.

In seasons of waiting for direction from God, we prefer pushing forward in the wrong direction over listening for His direction. But in doing that, we use up a lot of time and energy and find ourselves exhausted, not to mention too distracted to truly seek what God has for us next.

However, if we wait for the Lord to give us His direction, when we hear the gun go off at the starting line of the race, we will be ready to run and not grow weary. By resting in Him and finding peace in the clarity of His calling, we gain renewed strength in a world intent on circling the parking lot on empty.

Pray

Father, you know my tendency to rush ahead to do anything rather than wait patiently. Thank you for promising to guide me and for having a good plan for my life. Give me the perseverance to wait for your direction. Show me clearly what you want me to do. I'm listening.

Reflect

How am I moving in circles rather than waiting for the Lord today?

Day Eighteen

Wear Love

Four-year-old Maya and I have very different views on getting dressed. I have a mom "uniform" I wear practically every day. It is composed of jeans, tennis shoes, and a comfortable shirt that I have to change several times after getting spit up on. Jeans match everything, though, so changing the shirt is easy. At least that is my opinion. Maya disagrees.

She loves matching. In her opinion, jeans match nothing, except for maybe a jean shirt. In her world, the pants must match the shirt perfectly in color and pattern, therefore, jeans don't fit with anything in her wardrobe. And if she can't find the exact right article of clothing to match, she would rather not get dressed at all.

Read

Since God chose you to be the holy people he loves, you must clothe yourselves with tenderhearted mercy, kindness, humility, gentleness, and patience. Make allowance for each other's faults, and forgive anyone who offends you. Remember, the Lord forgave you, so you must forgive others. Above all, clothe yourselves with love, which binds us all together in perfect harmony. And let the peace that comes from Christ rule in your hearts. For as members of one body you are called to live in peace. And always be thankful.

Colossians 3:12-15a, NLT

Apply

Jesus teaches we should put on love like a well-worn, comfortable garment. It is the Christ-like response that matches any situation. Instead, we treat love with the same attitude that my daughter has towards jeans. We can come up with a lot of reasons it doesn't match our particular situation.

We can't love someone because they are different from us. They aren't sorry for what they did. They are infringing on our rights. They are trying to hurt us. We don't want to encourage whatever behavior they are exhibiting, so we withhold love, hoping that they will change and adopt our way of thinking. We don't have to love them until they match us.

Instead, Jesus says to wear love as the universal matching garment for every situation in the spirit of peace. We must choose to put on love, time after time, as the foundation of every interaction. We can dress it up or down, but over time, the stiff fabric that feels foreign and forced will mold our self-protection, pride, and judgment of others until love softens us and fits in all the right places.

Nothing in the world feels better than a broken-in pair of jeans. In the same way, when we make a habit of wearing love, there is nothing more beautiful in the kingdom of God.

Pray

Father, show me how I am withholding love. Let me rest in the knowledge of your love so that I can extend that love freely to others. Continue to help me choose love, even in the situations where love doesn't seem like a matching response.

Reflect

What is one situation in which I am choosing not to wear love?

Day Nineteen

Hiking in the Dark

Have you ever been hiking in the dark? It is a most unsettling experience. My husband and I were camping with some friends, and the campsite was down a one-mile trail from the parking spot. When we arrived at the trail head, it was long past sunset, and in the middle of the wilderness, the night was pitch black. In the palpable darkness, my ears compensated for what I couldn't see.

Every rustle in the bushes, every flap of wings, and every snapping twig seemed magnified. Pricking at the edges of my logic was the faintest whisper of fear. Fear of what, I don't know. That was exactly what I was afraid of—the unknown.

Not long into our trek, I asked Nathan to go ahead of me. This changed the entire experience. No longer carrying the burden of trying to stick to the hardly distinguishable path, I simply had to follow his lead. When he stopped, I stopped. When he said to duck under a branch, I ducked. When he said to step over a root, I lifted my foot a little higher. The fear melted away, and the hike took on a more adventurous atmosphere.

Read

Whenever the cloud lifted from above the tent, the Israelites set out; wherever the cloud settled, the Israelites encamped. At the Lord's command the Israelites set out, and at his command they encamped. As long as the cloud stayed over the tabernacle, they remained in camp. When the cloud remained over the tabernacle a long time, the Israelites obeyed the Lord's order and did not set out.

Numbers 9:17-19, NIV

Apply

I love how clearly God leads the Israelites. There are no maps, no pros and cons lists, no middle of the night pacing, and no series of goals. The Israelites have one job, and that is to follow. When the cloud lifts, they pack up. When the cloud rests, they stay put. Wherever the cloud goes, they follow. Wherever the cloud stops, they call home. God doesn't offer explanations or timelines. He is training His people to follow in absolute obedience. Can following God really be this simple?

Yes, and no. It isn't easy to live in uncertainty, never knowing when or where we might be going. It isn't easy to trust God completely and follow Him without question. When we can't see what is ahead, behind, or beside us, we become more attuned to God's voice. Looking at our surroundings through the light of the Bible, we can move forward in faith. This is the reliance that God desires from us. He wants every ounce of our focus fixed on Him.

Thankfully, He doesn't leave us to discern the path on our own. He gives us the Holy Spirit as a guide to warn us of the places to avoid, point out the path to follow, and go before us on our journey. All we have to do is follow.

Pray

Father, thank you for leading me and giving me the Holy Spirit as a guide. Help me keep my gaze fixed on you as I venture into dark and unknown places. Give me the courage to follow you without question or fear.

Reflect

In what decision do I need to follow God's lead?

Day Twenty

Dancing into Transition

In college, I spent four to eight hours a week swing dancing. Learning to dance was a clumsy process but well worth the practice. The problem is that, as a natural leader, I am a terrible follower, and following your dance partner's lead is the first lesson.

The best way to learn how to follow is to change partners regularly. Dancing with only one person makes me an expert at following their lead until eventually I'm not really following at all. I simply know their moves and do them without waiting for the lead. Switching partners keeps me sharp as a follower, constantly learning new variations of moves and how to respond to a variety of leading styles.

Now that I am married, I don't switch partners. My husband and I have spent countless hours dancing together over the years. When my husband and I dance together, it is difficult to know if I am really following, or simply reading his mind, imperceptibly sensing his next move based on past repetition. It looks seamless to a bystander, but my dance partner knows when I am taking the lead.

Read

The Lord had said to Abram, "Go from your country, your people and your father's household to the land I will show you. I will make you into a great nation, and I will bless you; I will make your name great, and you will be a blessing. I will bless those who bless you, and whoever curses you I will curse; and all peoples on earth will be blessed through you."

Genesis 12:1-3, NIV

Apply

When God calls Abraham, He basically tells him to leave everything established and familiar in his life and go to some other land, which is going to be a surprise. "I'll let you know when you get there." Have you ever been in a wonderful place in life and sensed God calling you to something new? Why does God initiate these pivots in life just when everything seems to be going fine?

Just like with dancing, when things are going smoothly and we are in our comfort zone, it is difficult to discern whether we are truly following God's lead or our own because the two are so indistinguishable. When we stay in one place for a long time, we learn that role so well that we don't realize our imperceptible decline in actual following. God wants us to depend completely on Him, which often requires a change of scenery.

On the other side of our decision to obey, there is a blessing! God may be vague about His instructions for Abraham, but He is specific with His promise for the future. When we take God's call to transition with obedient action, we receive the future blessings that He has planned for us as well.

Pray

Father, as difficult as it is to leave the familiar and make a change, give me the courage to say yes to whatever you have for me. Give me your peace and clarity as I move forward in obedience.

Reflect

When was the last time God asked me to make a change? Was I obedient? What was the outcome?

Day Twenty-One

The Finisher

Parenting has some grueling aspects. One of those is the necessity of finishing what I start. It means telling my daughter that we are going to sit at the table until she finishes all of her food, even if it means we have to sit there all night. My daughter knows that what I start, I will finish, because I love her, and eating her protein is going to help her grow.

Finishing means telling my toddler that I will help her clean her room, but we will not do anything else until we finish picking up. She groans, and whines, and drags her feet, and puts away each item at a sloth-like pace. But we keep at it until she finishes, because I love her.

Read

Being confident of this, that he who began a good work in you will carry it on to completion until the day of Christ Jesus.

Philippians 1:6, NIV

No discipline seems pleasant at the time, but painful. Later on, however, it produces a harvest of righteousness and peace for those who have been trained by it.

Hebrews 12:11, NIV

Apply

I never realized the application of the verse above until I became a mom. When I am in a season of struggle or pain, my achiever mindset draws conclusions for efficiently navigating God's discipline. I think, *Oh, I'm supposed to be learning a lesson. Let me figure out what that is, show God that I have learned it, and then we can move on.* Unfortunately, God isn't as concerned about what we learn as much as who we become.

I'm not making my daughter eat her food so that she learns to appreciate meat. I want her to develop gratitude for the meal. We don't clean her room so that she will have good house-keeping skills one day. She needs to learn responsibility for her things and develop a mindset of good stewardship. Likewise, if we learn the "lesson" but don't experience a change within the core of our souls, we have missed the purpose of the process.

God's goal is to draw us to Himself, and we accomplish that through faithfully following Him in obedience and trust. This is not a skill that we learn once and can add to our resume. This is character development that happens over time, through continual cycles of waiting on the Lord and watching Him faithfully provide. In time, we learn we can trust Him because He is unchanging.

If God says He will complete what He has started in us, we know He will be at our side, working out the weaknesses in our character for as long as it takes. He will never give up on us.

Pray

Father, thank you for loving me enough to commit to completing the good work you have started in me. Give me your strength and endurance to not only learn the lessons that you have for me, but to become the person who you want me to be.

Reflect

In what way is God currently working to make me more Christ-like?

Day Twenty-Two

Discipline over Punctuality

With strong-willed toddlers, much of my role as a parent involves teaching them right from wrong, creating boundaries, and endlessly reinforcing those boundaries with consistent consequences. This is by far the most time-consuming aspect of motherhood, but it is also the most important in this stage of their development.

As we were leaving for a birthday party this week, my toddler launched into a tantrum. I drove back into the garage, got out of the car, and took my daughter inside. We reviewed her actions and discussed what she could have done differently. With my daughter agreeing to behave within the boundaries, we resumed our drive to the party, now fashionably late.

Being on time is not the priority for me with my daughter's behavior. Making sure that she grows into an adult who loves the Lord and knows how to obey Him is more important than arriving on time.

Read

"My son, do not make light of the Lord's discipline, and do not lose heart when he rebukes you, because the Lord disciplines the one he loves, and he chastens everyone he accepts as his son." Endure hardship as discipline; God is treating you as his children. For what children are not disciplined by their father? If you are not disciplined—and everyone undergoes discipline—then you are not legitimate, not true sons and daughters at all. Moreover, we have all had human fathers who disciplined us and we respected them for it. How much more should we submit to the Father of spirits and live! They disciplined us for a little while as they thought best; but God disciplines us for our good, in order that we may share in his holiness. No discipline seems pleasant at the time, but painful. Later on, however, it produces a harvest of righteousness and peace for those who have been trained by it.

Hebrews 12:5b-11, NIV

Apply

Just as I discipline my daughter out of love, God does the same with us. Not only will God discipline us in love so that we become more like Christ, but He will take as long as necessary to accomplish His work. He is not in a hurry, and our delayed or canceled plans are not His top priority.

We seem to always give discipline a negative connotation, but I love how these verses relate discipline to training. In the same way that an athlete trains or a scholar studies, we must practice obedience to Christ. Seasons of waiting are exercises in patience. God will do whatever it takes to develop skills of patient love in us, no matter how long it takes, because we are His children, and He loves us.

Pray

Father, thank you for loving me enough to discipline me. Help me see your correction as a blessing rather than inconvenience or hardship. I want the harvest of righteousness that it will develop in time.

Reflect

In what ways do I treat God's discipline as a hardship to endure rather than a blessing given out of love?

Day Twenty-Three

Preparing the Nursery

One of my favorite parts of being pregnant is preparing the nursery. For all three of my daughters, I ordered custom fabric and sewed their nursery essentials myself. They each have a set of matching sheets, crib skirts, changing pad covers, curtains, throw pillows, blankets, and quilts. I searched for countless hours on the internet to pick out the perfect fabric for each of them and countless more hours sewing the unique pieces to prepare for their arrival.

As a planner, I had the crib set up, the clothes folded and put in the dresser drawers, and the closet stocked with organized bins of baby essentials months before their due dates. I ordered custom artwork for the walls with their names and Bible verses.

I have such fond memories of those quiet moments in the empty nursery, praying over them and dreaming of the day when my new baby would share it with me. I spend so much energy on perfecting the environment, but all I really want is to finally be with my new child.

Read

"Do not let your hearts be troubled. You believe in God; believe also in me. My Father's house has many rooms; if that were not so, would I have told you that I am going there to prepare a place for you? And if I go and prepare a place for you, I will come back and take you to be with me that you also may be where I am. You

know the way to the place where I am going."
Thomas said to him, "Lord, we don't know where you are going, so how can we know the way?"
Jesus answered, "I am the way and the truth and the life. No one comes to the Father except through me."

John 14:1-6, NIV

Apply

Our Father in Heaven is preparing a place for us at this very moment. He is planning for our arrival with great anticipation. He is adding personal touches to welcome us to our new home and is eagerly looking forward to the day when we will join Him in the paradise He has completed for us.

With the same love that we experience when we look forward to the birth of our own children, He is waiting expectantly for you. In the same way that my babies could not comprehend the amazing world they would be born into, there are no words to explain to us how incredible our arrival in heaven will be. We can only trust that our Father has given great attention to every detail and is longing to share it with us!

And the best part won't be the streets of gold, but the fact that we will be together with Him at last. This is the moment He is waiting for!

Pray

Father, thank you for the love and care that you put into preparing heaven for me! Help me rest, knowing that reaching heaven will be a joyful, long-awaited reunion with you.

Reflect

How does this view of heaven change my perspective towards everyday life on earth?

Day Twenty-Four

Switch Your Shoes

Four-year-old Maya loves to get dressed by herself, including putting on her shoes. While it would seem like she would mix up the right and left shoes fifty percent of the time, she has a one hundred percent track record of putting her shoes on the wrong feet. She considers the shoes carefully, and without fail, puts the left shoe on the right foot and vice-versa. In her mind, this is how they should go. And don't try to convince her otherwise!

Every day we have the same conversation:

"Maya, your shoes are on the wrong feet."

"I like them like this."

"Your feet will hurt if you wear them on the wrong feet."

"They don't hurt. This is fine."

"Okay. When your feet are hurting later, switch your shoes."

Then, throughout the day, I'll notice her feet bothering her until she eventually takes off her shoes and swaps feet.

Read

Repent, then, and turn to God, so that your sins may be wiped out, that times of refreshing may come from the Lord.

Acts 3:19, NIV

Apply

I may roll my eyes at Maya's determination to go her own way, but I am so much like her. Choosing to go our own way instead of God's is a daily occurrence in life, and it comes naturally. We study the choices before us, knowing right from wrong, and choose the self-serving path anyway.

We choose to return a differing opinion on social media with our own scathing response (whether or not we hit "post"), we lose our temper with our family members, we gossip or judge those around us internally, and the list goes on. Even when the Holy Spirit taps us on the shoulder and lets us know we are wrong and need to make a change, we often decide that we prefer to act this way.

But choosing our own way over God's way results in pain. It causes division and arguing. It creates a critical spirit that criticizes others and also ourselves, and it causes irreparable damage to the relationships that we care about the most. Eventually we sheepishly admit that our way is not best, tire of the resulting pain, and repent. Repent literally means to turn around. Let us remember that pain is an indicator that we need to take off our shoes and switch feet.

Pray

Father, thank you for putting pain in my life as a reminder to evaluate my actions. Give me the wisdom to listen to the Holy Spirit's prompting the first time, rather than choosing my own way. Most of all, thank you for offering unending forgiveness when I decide to turn back to you.

Reflect

In what way do I have my shoes on the wrong feet this week? What pain has it caused?

Day Twenty-Five

A Hard Freeze

We recently had a hard freeze, which is a rare occurrence for South Louisiana. Layers of ice covered everything for days. I realize this is normal for many places, but it was historic for us. As a gardener, I watched in dismay as my spring plants, with fresh green leaves poking out in every direction, curled back under the attack. The leaves folded in on themselves, their color draining away until only lifeless, brittle, brown foliage remained.

Once the ice melted, I spent days cutting back the bare branches, pulling out clumps of dead masses which were once the most hopeful spring tendrils. The bare ground left where so many varieties once flourished made me wonder if any of the plants would survive.

I watered, mulched, and waited. And as sure as the sun continues to rise, the plants which had completely disappeared unfurled fresh leaves from the soil. Bulbs unseen beneath the ground pushed up new buds, stretching for the light once again. New life! Not only did the plants return, they grew better than they had any previous year.

Read

We are hard pressed on every side, but not crushed; perplexed, but not in despair; persecuted, but not abandoned; struck down, but not destroyed. We always carry around in our body the death of Jesus, so that the life of Jesus may also be revealed in our body.

For we who are alive are always being given over to death for Jesus' sake, so that his life may also be revealed in our mortal body. So then, death is at work in us, but life is at work in you.

2 Corinthians 4:8-12, NIV

Apply

In life, there are hardships that blow in unexpectedly, like a hard freeze. An illness, a loss, a season of grief, or a struggle can drain all the color from our lives. Pain can leave our bodies and souls brittle and bare. It is easy to wonder if signs of life will ever return.

This loss is part of life on this broken earth. It is unavoidable. And yet, we carry within us, deep below the barren soil of our hearts, the incredible new life of Christ. Even after the most difficult of storms, nothing can stop the new life that He gives from creeping up out of the soil once more.

He is making all things new. He is the true Gardener. From the dark places of silence, weakness, and brokenness, He lifts our chin and reminds us that He is the Author of redemption and reconciliation. He will not only bring back what was lost but also recreate a thriving, beautiful garden of hope and new life.

Pray

Father, thank you for never leaving my side when the storms of life threaten to steal my hope and joy. Thank you for being a patient and faithful gardener that continues to grow new life in me. Help me rest in you during the seasons of bare soil, knowing that you have not finished working in me.

Reflect

What set of circumstances feels like a hard freeze in my life right now?

Day Twenty-Six

Vain Name

When I was expecting my second daughter, I wanted a sign of her name in cursive to hang over the crib. The price for buying a wooden sign was more than I wanted to pay, so I made my own. As a toddler mom with free time at a premium, I spent every night for several weeks tracing out the letters in loopy font on a thick foam core board, painstakingly cutting it out with a craft knife, patiently sanding down the rough edges, and finally painting it a perfect shade of lavender to coordinate with the nursery. It came out beautiful — truly magazine-worthy.

A few weeks later, I carefully brought the name with us as a prop for our family baby bump pictures. During the photo shoot, my then eighteen-month-old launched into an epic tantrum and destroyed the beautiful name I had created. On the way home, I was devastated, carrying the foam core board in a pile of pieces in my lap. The baby I created it for would never see it.

Read

You shall not misuse the name of the LORD your God, for the LORD will not hold anyone guiltless who misuses his name.

Exodus 20:7, NIV

I tell you, on the day of judgment people will give account for every careless word they speak, for by your words you will be justified, and by your words you will be condemned.

Matthew 12:36-37, ESV

Apply

I used to think that this verse was talking about saying the name of God next to a curse word, and the consequence of such an innocent slip seemed harsh. In reality, taking God's name in vain is so much more. God has worked tirelessly to present His name as one that is based in love, trustworthy at all times, and unchanging no matter the circumstances.

As Christians, we bear the name of "Christ" in everything that we do. We essentially carry around His beautiful name and reputation, which He has hand-crafted and proven over eternity. When others see us in everyday life, they connect His name to our actions like a prop in a photo shoot.

Therefore, when we have days that end in our own adult version of a tantrum, we are taking His name and all that it represents and breaking it into pieces in view of everyone around us. No wonder so many people mistrust God's name and character, when we so often destroy it in public with our own selfish actions.

We have all broken this commandment. And yet, God calls us His children. He gives us the right to bear His name and allows us to call Him Father. As Christ followers, let us never take our namesake for granted.

Pray

Father, thank you for having a character that is trustworthy and proven. Help me display your legacy of love to others in a way that draws them to your name rather than giving them a reason to turn away. Help me represent you well in everything that I do.

Reflect

How have I misused God's name by my poor example? How can I better represent the holiness of God's name in my everyday life?

Day Twenty-Seven

A Change of Perspective

Dinner time is one of the most stressful in my house. Depending on my husband's work schedule, I am sometimes on my own for getting the girls fed. This sounds fine in theory, but having two bouncy toddlers who would rather flit about the room makes it a challenge.

It's as futile as herding cats, attempting to wrangle them into their chairs long enough to get a few bites in before they bound back off. Their eating attention span lasts approximately 1.6 seconds. It doesn't help that I am tired after a long day and ready for a break by dinnertime. I relegate to barking orders and giving snippy responses.

After several months of dreading this hour of the day, I made a change. I usually sit in the chair with my back to the window, but I moved to the opposite side of the table. From this new vantage point, I can look out of the window at the flowers bursting from the backyard garden. The change made an immediate difference. Seeing the flowers and sunshine puts me in a better mood, which allows me to act with more patience towards the girls.

I point out interesting things outside to the girls. "Look at that butterfly! And there's a little bird sitting on that branch. Can you see it?" As they focus on the beauty out the window, the girls stay in their chairs and eat rather than hopping off the nearest distraction.

Read

Finally, brothers and sisters, whatever is true, whatever is noble, whatever is right, whatever is pure, whatever is lovely, whatever is admirable—if anything is excellent or praiseworthy—think about such things.

Philippians 4:8, NIV

Apply

In moving to a new chair, my circumstances didn't change. I had the same task of feeding two toddlers at the same time of day, when we all possessed the least amount of patience. The only thing that changed was my point of view. Instead of focusing on my frustration, I took pleasure in the little things that I could be grateful for. As a result, it changed the girls' focus as well.

We must choose to live in such a way that we intentionally focus on something good, no matter how difficult the circumstances are. We must re-position ourselves to express gratitude rather than frustration. When we choose to change our perspective in this way, it is amazing how God can use the smallest blessings to counteract the most stressful parts of life.

Pray

Father, thank you for giving me something to be grateful for, no matter how frustrating my circumstances are. Help me focus on what you have blessed me with so that I can gain new insight in seasons of strain.

Reflect

How can I re-position my life to focus on God's blessings with gratitude?

Day Twenty-Eight

Matching Breath

A fussy, overtired baby is a thing to behold. The other night, my six-month-old had reached her limit. Though exhausted, she wouldn't settle down to nap. I rocked her and tried to snuggle her, but she cried and fought and struggled and grunted.

Fighting the urge to feed off of her frustration, I held her tight, leaned back in the rocker and took slow, relaxing deep breaths. Eventually her tight little fists loosened, her head relaxed against my chest, and her quick, shallow breathing slowed to match my own.

She allowed her warm head to rest against me, wispy baby hair pressed against my cheek. We breathed in together. We breathed out together. As she finally surrendered to sleep, her weighted limbs draped over me, and she rested.

Read

Come to me, all you who are weary and burdened, and I will give you rest.

Matthew 11:28, NIV

In peace I will lie down and sleep, for you alone, Lord, make me dwell in safety.

Psalm 4:8, NIV

In vain you rise early and stay up late, toiling for food to eat— for he grants sleep to those he loves.

Psalm 127:2, NIV

Apply

Can you relate to an overtired baby as much as I can? We get stressed, worked up, exhausted, and frustrated. When God calls us to rest in Him, we fight it, insisting that there is still so much that we need to take care of.

In the same way that I know my child needs rest, God knows that surrender is more necessary than finishing all the tasks on our to do list. He offers to take the weight of everything that we are carrying, but there is a catch. In order for us to find our rest in Him, we must be with Him.

We must be in His presence, allow Him to place our head on His chest, listen to the pace of His breathing, and surrender our will to Him. Before God can carry our burdens, we must release them. Instead of fighting His call to submit, let us choose to rest in His safety and trust His provision and love.

Pray

Father, thank you for offering rest for my soul. Thank you for not giving this rest from far away, but in a close and intimate relationship with me. Give me the courage to release my burdens with faith that you will take care of them and me.

Reflect

What burden am I carrying today that God is asking me to release to Him?

Day Twenty-Nine

The Great Artist

My four-year-old, Maya, is an artist. Her room is full of craft supplies, and she is always diligently creating something. Doing a project with her is practically impossible because she painstakingly controls every detail of the design.

When making Valentines for her classmates, she thinks of each friend and chooses a color that fits their personality. She writes their name in a font that suits their style and adds embellishments that match their preferences.

I am sure that the child receiving each Valentine has no notion of the care and effort that Maya puts into each small decision in her creation. But I can guarantee there is no minor detail in her work that isn't carefully considered and chosen with purpose.

Read

When I look at your heavens, the work of your fingers, the moon and the stars, which you have set in place, what is man that you are mindful of him, and the son of man that you care for him?
Psalm 8:3-4, NIV

The Lord wraps himself in light as with a garment; he stretches out the heavens like a tent and lays the beams of his upper chambers on their waters. He makes the clouds his chariot and rides on the wings of the wind.
Psalm 104:2-3, NIV

Apply

Our creative ability comes from the greatest Artist of all: God. So often I look at nature with awe but don't consider the thought process of God while creating it. Since God simply spoke and things appeared, I falsely assume that creation wasn't a carefully detailed process.

One look at any created thing will prove otherwise. What a mystery of how seeds grow into plants! What remarkable beauty that each created thing is unique, from the smallest snowflake to the massive stars. What an astounding miracle how babies grow in their mother's wombs!

From the smallest molecule to the expanse of the universe, the evidence of God's careful order and purpose in creation is overwhelming. His creation is a personal Valentine to us, an expression of His deep love. In the same way that Maya's friends will never know the full effort that went into her creations for them, we can never fully appreciate the vast complexity of God's creation.

Even more unbelievable is that His most prized creation is you and me. What a mystery to be so loved, so carefully designed, and so cared for by the Creator of the universe!

Pray

Father, thank you for the immeasurable care that you put into every piece of creation that I see each day. Thank you for the meaning and purpose behind each color and design. When I see the complexity of nature, help me remember how much you care for me. Allow me to live out my purpose so that I can bring you glory.

Reflect

How does appreciating God's creation change how I view myself?

Day Thirty

Fat Freedom!

The week before Christmas this past year, I started having episodes of intense pain right below my ribs. It was quickly diagnosed as gallstones, and I scheduled my gall bladder removal surgery for mid-March. For the two and a half months before the surgery, I had to be extremely careful about what I ate in order to avoid having a gallbladder attack. I had to eat low-fat foods, so I quickly eliminated cheese, cream, nuts, avocados, red meat, and anything fried from my diet. I ate grilled chicken, fruits, vegetables, and bread for months. Changing my diet didn't cure the gallstones, but it did curb the painful side effects.

However, once my gallbladder was removed, I was free to eat anything I wanted. And let me tell you, freedom tastes so good! I can still choose to eat within my former dietary restrictions if I want to, but it would be for a new reason. I can eat low-fat food because it makes me feel good, helps me stay at a healthy weight, or fuels my body with the right nutrients to perform at its best. But avoiding fatty foods out of obligation would defeat the purpose of having the surgery, because the cause of pain is gone.

Read

It is for freedom that Christ has set us free. Stand firm, then, and do not let yourselves be burdened again by a yoke of slavery. Mark my words! I, Paul, tell you that if you let yourselves be circumcised, Christ will be of no value to you at all. You who are trying to be justified by the law have been alienated from Christ;

you have fallen away from grace. For through the Spirit we eagerly await by faith the righteousness for which we hope. For in Christ Jesus neither circumcision nor uncircumcision has any value. The only thing that counts is faith expressing itself through love.

Galatians 5:1-2,4-6, NIV

Apply

Ever since the first sin in the Garden of Eden, we have had the curse of sin inside of us, a separation we can't resolve. Following God's law in the Old Testament didn't solve the problem of sin but allowed us to avoid the painful consequences temporarily. Following the law was a short-term solution until the sin could be removed completely. When Jesus died on the cross and rose again, He paid the eternal consequence for our actions. When we accept His gift of forgiveness, He doesn't merely cover up or ignore our sins; He removes them. He has set us free!

In the verses above, Paul is addressing the issue of circumcision, but the same idea of freedom can apply to any law in society or the church. He explains that following the law is no longer our chief concern. What matters is the reasoning behind the choice. We can choose to follow laws out of love and sensitivity to others, out of respect for God, or for personal benefit. But following the law out of fear or obligation defeats the purpose of Jesus' sacrifice. He has set us free to live in the freedom of love.

Pray

Father, thank you for sending Jesus to take away my sin and set me free from striving, obligation, shame, and guilt. Show me any areas of my life in which I am enslaving myself to a law instead of embracing the freedom of Christ.

Reflect

What rules do I follow out of obligation rather than respect?

Day Thirty-One

The Treasure Room

When I was little, I loved to visit my grandmother's house. She was a collector, and she had a spare bedroom that was filled to the brim with her treasures. She had teacups and saucers from countries around the world, porcelain dolls in all shapes and sizes, antique furniture, delicately painted glassware, and vintage hats. There were boxes filled with unknown treasures stacked as high as possible in every nook and cranny of the room, with only a small walkway to shimmy through.

To a seven-year-old girl, this usually off-limits room was incredibly fascinating. I loved to walk through the room with my grandmother. She would stop at each item and give me the long story about what made it special. She would linger lovingly over each item, her prized possessions.

Read

Do not store up for yourselves treasures on earth, where moths and vermin destroy, and where thieves break in and steal. But store up for yourselves treasures in heaven, where moths and vermin do not destroy, and where thieves do not break in and steal. For where your treasure is, there your heart will be also.

Matthew 6:19-21, NIV

Apply

We know earthly treasures will pass away, but what do treasures in heaven really comprise? We tend to think that treasures in heaven comprise our gifts to others or a collection of our good deeds. However, God says in I Samuel 15:22 that He desires obedience more than offerings or sacrifices. This means that our treasure in heaven is not equivalent to the amount that we "pay it forward" in this life but the amount that we submit our own will to God's will.

In our society, obedience is an under-valued trait. While our Western culture hails independence, ingenuity, and self-sufficiency as strengths, the Bible asserts that obedience, humility, and dependence on God ought to be our chief virtues.

Obedience means forgiving others when they aren't sorry, instead of choosing to cling to my victim hood. It means willingly laying down my rights when I am justified in demanding them. It means acting with integrity, even when being honest could ruin my chances of reaching my goals.

My decision to obey or disobey in these situations reveals whether I value treasure in heaven or on earth. While we can never hold these heavenly treasures in our hands, they are more real and lasting than any we will ever gain on this side of heaven.

Pray

Father, give me discernment so that I can see earthly treasures and heavenly treasure for their true value. Help me to not lose sight of what truly matters in pursuit of something temporary. I trust you to know what is best, and I choose to value obedience to you over all else.

Reflect

What is one area of life in which I am choosing to value my earthly treasures over heavenly ones?

Day Thirty-Two

Green Tomatoes

Early summer is the most wonderful time of the year for the vegetable garden. With each rain, the plants surge toward the sun, fresh green shoots spreading in every direction. The flowers are fading on the plants, and tiny green fruits are appearing in their former place.

Growing vegetables is an incredible miracle. My older girls love to help me in the garden. At ages three and five, they are finally at an age where they can be more help than hindrance, unless they need patience.

No matter how many times I explain that we must wait until the tomatoes turn red before we pick them off of the plans, those tiny green spheres on the plant are just too much of a temptation. Given any time alone with the plants, the girls will pluck them all off.

As a result, I have a kitchen windowsill full of unripe and useless tomatoes. After all of our hard work growing the plants, we may not end up eating any tomatoes this year.

Read

Since ancient times no one has heard, no ear has perceived, no eye has seen any God besides you, who acts on behalf of those who wait for him.

Isaiah 64:4, NIV

Wait for the Lord; be strong, and let your heart take courage; wait for the Lord!

Psalm 27:14, ESV

Apply

As believers, we know God is growing us to be more like Him. He uses everything around us to draw us to Himself—His word, His creation, suffering and hardships, and unexpected blessings. So often I see something of His character beginning to grow in me, and I want it to be complete right away, without allowing Him to finish the work that He is doing.

I want the suffering to end, the lesson to be learned, the process to be finished without having to wait quietly in His presence and learn at His feet. In a culture where we celebrate *doing*, Jesus calls us to a life of *being*. And being takes patience.

In gardening, we plant, water, and weed, but ultimately God makes the plants grow and the fruit appear and ripen. If we want to enjoy the harvest, we must also be able to wait. In order to allow God to work in wondrous ways in and through us, we must wait and linger in the moment with Him, whether it is a moment of joy or pain. In learning to be still with Him, we give Him the time and space to act on our behalf in ways we could never imagine.

Pray

Father, I know my tendency is to act. Help me sit still in your presence, wait on your timing, and rely on your intervention. Show me how to harvest the character that you want for me by being patient in the ripening process.

Reflect

In what situation do I need to sit still and wait for God to act?

Day Thirty-Three

Party Planner

My very particular daughter just turned five. She wanted a rainbow birthday party, and since the previous year's celebration was subdued because of COVID, I went all out. Her most specific request was a six-layer rainbow cake that required six colors of frosting, six colors of cake, and six colors of fondant.

After working on this confectionery creation all day, she popped into the kitchen to check on my progress and scrutinized the fondant rainbow drying on the counter. I wait for her to "ooh" and "aah" over my handiwork. Instead, she scrunched up her nose.

"The last color in the rainbow is purple. That's brown."

I'm not perfect, especially with cake decorating, but this party was the most incredible rainbow explosion any five-year-old could ever dream of. Unfortunately, she couldn't fully enjoy her special day because of that one strip of fondant rainbow that wasn't exactly how she wanted it.

Read

My plans aren't your plans, nor are your ways my ways, says the Lord. Just as the heavens are higher than the earth, so are my ways higher than your ways, and my plans than your plans.

Isaiah 55:8-9, NIV

We can make our own plans, but the Lord gives the right answer.

Proverbs 16:1, NLT

We can make our plans, but the Lord determines our steps.

Proverbs 16:9, NLT

Apply

While my daughter's response was frustrating, how many times have I had the same attitude towards the plans that God lays out for my life? I have my plans, and I think they are pretty good. But then God has His plans, and they are very different.

I try hard to incorporate His plans into mine, but this only results in a frustrating and directionless, watered-down life. He plans an all-out technicolor celebration that includes not only our lives but weaves into all of eternity, impacting generations we will never know or see.

Our plans are worthless because they are short-sighted. We cannot see eternity. We cannot hold the universe in our hands. We cannot know the effect of our fleeting lives on this earth. But God does. He knows how all the pieces come together in the end, and that is why we can trust Him. What a tragedy if we allow an insignificant detail of life that doesn't go the way we wanted to keep us from the joy of serving God wholeheartedly with our lives.

Pray

Father, I know your plans are superior to mine. Give me the courage to follow you without hesitation, no matter how different your plan looks from my own ideas. Help me surrender any disappointing differences from what I had in mind, knowing that you know what is best for me.

Reflect

What unmet expectation is keeping me from embracing full obedience to God's will for my life?

Day Thirty-Four

Hurricane Baby

My third daughter was born in October under very exciting circumstances. Not only would she be a pandemic baby, but she would also be a hurricane baby. Her due date fell on the projected landfall of Hurricane Delta, and unlike either of my other babies, she arrived exactly on time. The day was very eventful, including pushing our kids out of the van at the curb of my parents' house, tossing out their luggage and the cat in the torrential downpour, and losing electricity at the hospital after arriving there already fully dilated. But those are stories for another day.

I had heard the rumors of birth being naturally induced during hurricanes but thought it an old wives' tale. However, a little research and personal experience have proven otherwise. The low pressure system in the hurricane causes women to go into labor.

A rain band would pass over, and my contractions would get closer together and more intense, and as the band left, they would ease up again and get further apart. It was a crazy sensation! The process continued until the pain finally ceased and sweet little Clara joined our family, and the whole crazy day was worth it.

Read

I consider that our present sufferings are not worth comparing with the glory that will be revealed in us. We know that the whole creation has been groaning as in the pains of childbirth right up to the present time. Not only so, but we ourselves, who have the firstfruits of the Spirit, groan inwardly as we wait eagerly for our adoption to sonship, the redemption of our bodies. For in this hope we were saved. But hope that is seen is no hope at all. Who hopes for what they already have? But if we hope for what we do not yet have, we wait for it patiently.

Romans 8:18, 22-25, NIV

Apply

While we are here on earth, we are experiencing waves of suffering, trials, and difficult circumstances. Even though these storms make our awareness of pain more acute and magnified, they also speed up the process of becoming like Christ. It is in these intense moments of difficulty that we make the most progress in our spiritual growth.

The intensity of contractions enables us to birth a child. In the same way, the hardships that we face in life, though painful, bring us closer to the Father's heart until finally, at just the right time, we meet Him face-to-face. And in that moment, all the pain and suffering of our journey will pale compared to the long-awaited reunion with Him. We will rejoice in the glory that He reveals in us, slowly refined and purified through the fires that we face today. Do not give up hope! Our pain is not without purpose.

Pray

Father, thank you for promising that you will use even the painful moments in life to create something beautiful and worth celebrating. Only you can take what is almost unbearable and use it for your good. Give me perseverance in times of suffering, knowing that the pain serves a purpose.

Reflect

What storms have helped me grow closer to Christ? In what ways has He used them to create something good?

Day Thirty-Five

Dead Seeds

We are growing green beans in our vegetable garden this year. I explained to the girls that when a green bean plant produces beans, it is doing so in order to make seeds that will grow new plants. It creates beans, not to produce food, but to ensure reproduction of the species before the mother plant dies.

Then my five-year-old wanted to plant every green bean pod we had picked. I had to clarify that in order for the seeds to sprout, they first have to die. We have to leave the pods on the plants until they turn brown and the seeds fall forgotten on the soil. Only then, after the seed gives up its life, does the root wiggle out and reach deep into the dirt and the stem pushes its way up toward the sun, creating a new plant.

Now when we are eating our green beans, my daughter asks, "Do you have any dead beans that we can plant?"

Read

Jesus replied, "The hour has come for the Son of Man to be glorified. Very truly I tell you, unless a kernel of wheat falls to the ground and dies, it remains only a single seed. But if it dies, it produces many seeds. Anyone who loves their life will lose it, while anyone who hates their life in this world will keep it for eternal life."

John 12:23-25, NIV

Apply

Oh, how painfully true this comparison is to life in Christ! We want meaning and purpose in our lives today. We believe that what we accomplish in our fleeting days on earth determines our worth in God's kingdom, but that is not true. Instead, what truly counts as gain is what we put to death.

Even with all the incredible ministry that Jesus did—healing the sick, raising the dead, and preaching to the masses—none of that resulted in His glorification. Scripture explains that the moment of His death was His victory. His ministry was good, but His death was life.

Likewise, our victory comes from what we lose. When we release dreams, sacrifice possessions, set aside our rights, surrender our position, and give away our time and energy, we waste away in the most noble manner. We lose everything and gain eternity. Like hardened seeds falling from their brittle pods, our poured out lives sprout into a new plant that produces far more than a lone vegetable on a fancy plate ever could. Would you rather be a single, tasty bean or a seed that in turn produces far more plants? God is asking, "Are there any people willing to die that I can use to build my Kingdom?"

Pray

Father, help me shift my focus from what I can achieve to what I can give away for your kingdom. Whether it is something physical (such as possessions), mental (such as a selfish or judgmental attitude), emotional (such as a dream or goal), or spiritual (such as a pattern of sin), help me put everything to death for you. I will take up my cross and die, knowing you bring life from death.

Reflect

What do I need to put to death today?

Day Thirty-Six

One More Snuggle

A staggering range of emotions come with having a newborn. With Clara just a few weeks old, she is awake for hours several times every night. I am often completely exhausted, unable to console, bounce, or cuddle her for one more minute. But to my dismay, just after I finally get her to sleep and collapse into bed, she startles and cries yet again.

Almost in tears, I plead with her, "Go to sleep. I'm done. I can't keep doing this all night." Pulling her away from my chest and looking down at her, I am overcome by her mere existence and flooded with love, "Oh my goodness, you are so cute! You are seriously the most adorable thing in the world."

And once again, unable to give even an ounce more of energy, "But, please, don't even think about waking up again until morning. I have to sleep." Her warm body relaxes into mine and her breathing evens out. She is finally asleep! (Again.) Before laying her down to rush to my bed in relief, I hesitate. Oh, it is so sweet just to hold her!

"I love you so much! I'm just going to smell your soft head one more time before I lay you down."

Read

You see, at just the right time, when we were still powerless, Christ died for the ungodly. Very rarely will anyone die for a righteous person, though for a good person someone might possibly dare to die. But God demonstrates his own love for us in this: While we were still sinners, Christ died for us.

Romans 5:6-8, NIV

Apply

It is easy to love babies even on their most arduous nights because of their powerlessness and innocence. No matter how terrible a baby's behavior or sleeplessness, motherly love will always overcome it. This reflects God's love for us.

We often think of God as a stern judge who lays down the law. In reality, He is a loving Father who lays down His Son's life. In the same way that my overwhelming love for Clara overshadows any disdain for her crying, God's love for us is no chore, even on our most rebellious days. His love for us is incomparable!

He truly, deeply loves us while also completely and ruthlessly detesting our sinful behavior. He loves us despite our actions, because He is love, and we are His children. Even while we were at our worst, even when He knew He could not stand our sin for a single moment more, He did not abandon us to our fate, but gave up His own Son to make a way for us to return to His embrace. Like an exhausted mother at the end of her endurance, He still wants one more snuggle from a most undeserving child.

Pray

Father, thank you for loving me more than I could ever imagine. Thank you that this love is not because of anything that I have done but because of who you are, and therefore unconditional. I am sorry for my sinful behaviors that create distance in our relationship. Thank you for the gift of forgiveness that you offer through Jesus. Help me to always turn back to you.

Reflect

How does the truth of God's love change my view of Him?

Day Thirty-Seven

Vacation ER

On our family vacation, the planned schedule deteriorates almost immediately. The first night in the hotel, our three-year-old rolls out of bed and is awake for the next five hours in pain. At the ER the following morning, Nathan and I have a quick parent huddle.

It went something like this: "No matter what happens today, everything is going to be fun. This is our vacation, and it is all a splendid adventure."

We are not feeling fun or adventurous. We are feeling exhausted and worried. But we make a conscious decision to keep the day positive for the kids. We make the snack counter seem like a feast, the x-ray like a photo shoot, and the emergency room like a children's museum.

One diagnosed broken collarbone and an arm sling later, we are back to having fun for real. The rest of our trip truly is fantastic, even when lots of little things don't go how we planned. Somehow, our decision to enjoy the time together, no matter the circumstances, transforms our joy from a forced effort to a genuine sentiment.

Read

Though the fig tree does not bud and there are no grapes on the vines, though the olive crop fails and the fields produce no food, though there are no sheep in the pen and no cattle in the stalls, yet I will rejoice in the Lord, I will be joyful in God my Savior. The

Sovereign Lord is my strength; he makes my feet like the feet of a deer, he enables me to tread on the heights.

Habakkuk 3:17-19, NIV

Apply

These verses give clear direction about how we should react when faced with difficult situations: rejoicing. Not only are we to not complain, but to take it a big step further, we are called to react with joy. This reaction is contrary to everything that we naturally feel at the moment. It is a conscious decision that we must choose to make, regardless of the circumstances.

When life is difficult, rejoice in the Lord. When things feel out of control, rejoice in the Lord. When the future is uncertain, rejoice in the Lord. When the blessing you asked for turns out to be an overwhelming responsibility, rejoice in the Lord.

While these verses begin with what seems like a forced decision to praise God, the effort quickly turns into a genuine sentiment of thanksgiving, acknowledging the amazing things God does to redeem our darkest moments. While choosing joy at first seems like an obligation, we can't help but end with a result of genuine gratitude and rejoicing. Whatever you face, rejoice in the Lord always!

Pray

Father, thank you for giving me strength to choose joy in even the most difficult circumstance in life. Give me a heart that finds joy in your presence, regardless of my feelings at the moment. Transform my heart and mind into a lifestyle of praise and devotion.

Reflect

What set of circumstances do I need to choose to rejoice in today?

Day Thirty-Eight

At the Threshold

I am standing awkwardly outside the door to my parents' house. The door is open, my dad standing inside with a welcoming smile and a gesture to walk inside. Instead, I hesitate. It seems as if there is an invisible wall at the threshold that I cannot force myself to cross. Though unseen, this barrier is real. It is June 2020, and I haven't been in a building other than my home in three months, and the facts about COVID are still uncertain.

Why can't I seem to step across the space between my dad and me? That's easy. What if I have unknowingly contracted COVID, and I infect my parents? Would they resent me for exposing them? Would I be able to live with the guilt if something happened? Risk vs. reward: is this short visit worth their possible death? A love for my parents, coupled with a selfish desire to avoid blame, keeps me from strolling casually through the open door. Once I cross the threshold and enter the house, I make a decision to take responsibility for whatever comes next.

Read

The judgment followed one sin and brought condemnation, but the gift followed many trespasses and brought justification. For if, by the trespass of the one man, [Adam,] death reigned through that one man, how much more will those who receive God's abundant provision of grace and of the gift of righteousness reign in life through the one man, Jesus Christ!

Romans 5:16b-17, NIV (brackets added for context)

Apply

Our heavenly Father gives us the same invitation that my dad did. He is standing with the doors to righteousness open, a welcoming smile on His face, beckoning us to come. And yet, even with forgiveness for our sins freely offered, so many times we hesitate to run into His embrace. We stand so close, yet remain on the other side of an unseen and formidable barrier. Why don't we go to God with our failures and mistakes? That's easy. In the presence of His perfection, our own sin becomes glaringly apparent. It isn't a question of whether we are infected; we know we are sinners.

We fear God will resent us for not measuring up, and Jesus' death on the cross to offer us forgiveness only piles on the guilt. We feel the pressure to live up to Jesus' sacrifice, to make ourselves someone worth dying for. Inevitably we come up short, and not wanting to take blame for what we have done, we keep our distance.

What we don't understand is that our sin has already "infected" Jesus. He took it on Himself and died as a result. But we don't need to carry the weight of that sacrifice, because He conquered sin and death with His resurrection. There is no resentment on His part. It is an action that He took willingly, knowing that we could never deserve it. The moment we try to earn His forgiveness, we undermine the power of His grace.

Pray

Father, thank you for offering forgiveness through Jesus. Help me overcome thoughts of guilt and blame that come with sin. Free me from striving to earn your love. Let me run to you today, confessing all of my shortcomings, and embracing the forgiveness and grace that you offer.

Reflect

How and why have I been keeping my distance from God?

Day Thirty-Nine

Goggle Vision

The girls love to play with diving rings in the swimming pool. As they were playing the other day, I noticed they were getting all the colors wrong.

"Get that purple one," Maya would say, pointing to a blue one.

"Here's the orange one!" Everly would beam, holding up a yellow one.

At first I wondered if this was some kind of complicit game because they weren't correcting one another. I seemed to be the only one who disagreed. I continued to puzzle over this for a while, and when I realized the answer, I had to laugh.

The girls were wearing their swimming goggles to dive and get the toys. In true girl style, their goggles have pink lenses, which affects their perception of the colors of everything around them. Neither of them noticed that anything was out of the ordinary because they were both seeing the same distorted colors.

Read

Do not conform to the pattern of this world, but be transformed by the renewing of your mind. Then you will be able to test and approve what God's will is—his good, pleasing and perfect will.

Romans 12:2, NIV

Apply

Have you ever wondered why it is so difficult to figure out what God's will is? It is because of our "goggle vision." Living in the world distorts our view away from God's perspective, and this phenomenon happens collectively. A lens through which a culture views life slowly tints over time until the entire group clearly agrees that something is what it truly isn't. We don't even realize our mistaken perspective because it is the same as those around us.

We can only see our circumstances and decisions as they truly are when we take on the un-tinted perspective of God. When we read His Word and ask for His wisdom, He removes the colored lenses from our eyes and allows us to see with the crisp clarity that He does. Our distorted lenses in life allow us to excuse sinful patterns, regularly entertain judgmental thoughts, and perpetuate harmful habits. Our own motives and goals of success, pride, happiness, and reputation obscure God's desires for us.

God's goals are far different. It is only when we allow Him to take off our tainted mindset that we see the beauty in His good plans for us, which are often marked by far different characteristics: pain, patience, loss, and surrender.

Pray

Father, thank you for not only having a godly perspective of my life, but for making good plans for me from that eternal view. Help me see my life from your view and not the world's. Transform my mind and renew my heart.

Reflect

In what way am I resisting God's will because it doesn't fit my perspective? What distorted view does that reveal?

Day Forty

Daily Milk

When my nine-month-old wakes up in the middle of the night with a pang of hunger, she expects me to walk in the room. For the last 270 nights, I have answered her middle-of-the-night cries for food, care, and comfort. We have a reliable breastfeeding routine of snuggling close every handful of hours for a quiet, shared embrace that refuels her physically, emotionally, and socially.

She knows where her sustenance comes from, and she relaxes when I am near. Her entire life relies on my consistent provision for her, so as soon as I step away, she gets anxious. If she can't see me, am I still there? Where will she get her next meal?

It is hard for me to not ask, "When have I ever abandoned you? Have I ever given you a reason to worry?" If only my proven track record could give her security for the future! But then again, she's only a baby.

Read

Then Jesus declared, "I am the bread of life. Whoever comes to me will never go hungry, and whoever believes in me will never be thirsty. But as I told you, you have seen me and still you do not believe. All those the Father gives me will come to me, and whoever comes to me I will never drive away."

John 6:35-37, NIV

The faithful love of the Lord never ends! His mercies never cease. Great is his faithfulness; his mercies begin afresh each morning. I say to myself, "The Lord is my inheritance; therefore, I will hope in him!"

Lamentations 3:22-24, NLT

Apply

One of the character traits that I most appreciate about God is His constancy, His reliability, His unchanging nature. Throughout the Bible, we see Him provide over and over without fail, and we know He is the same God today that He is in the Bible. Yet when a need arises in our present lives, we still seem to look around with our hands in the air, wondering where we can get some help.

Thankfully, instead of losing patience with our inability to put our faith in His provision, God sent us a physical manifestation of Himself in Christ to show His reliability more fully. Jesus' life, death, and resurrection give a beautiful, sacrificial, and permanent demonstration of His commitment to provide for us.

We can reliably on Him to refuel us physically, spiritually, and emotionally. When troubles arise, we don't have to wonder where our help comes from. He is our Bread of Life.

Pray

Father, thank you for your consistent provision since before time began. Help me replace anxiety, doubt, and worry with faith in your care for me. Remind me to run to you when I hunger or thirst, whether my need is physical, spiritual, or emotional. Thank you for giving me confidence that you will always be my fulfillment.

Reflect

What need can I surrender to God's provision today?

Day Forty-One

Swimming Lessons

My older girls (ages five and three) take swimming lessons. My five-year-old learned to swim last summer and insists that she does not need to take lessons again this year because she already knows how to swim. While she can successfully make it across the pool without drowning, there is still a lot that she can learn and practice. I could not could convince her that more training was necessary. On her first lesson, she explained her mastery of swimming to the coach, who nodded and tried to hide a grin.

"Show me what you know to prove you don't need to be here," was the teacher's wise reply.

Maya swam her very best and worked hard throughout her lesson. After each skill, the swim teacher showed her new techniques, pushed her a little farther, and even taught her a new stroke. I asked Maya if she was looking forward to her next lesson.

"Yes! I wonder what new thing I am going to learn next time."

That is a girl who has learned that there is always more to learn.

Read

Let us draw near to God with a sincere heart and with the full assurance that faith brings, having our hearts sprinkled to cleanse us from a guilty conscience and having our bodies washed with pure water. Let us hold unswervingly to the hope we profess, for he who promised is faithful. And let us consider how we may spur one another on toward love and good deeds, not giving up meeting together, as some are in the habit of doing, but encouraging one another—and all the more as you see the Day approaching.

Hebrews 10:22-25, NIV

Apply

It is easy as a Christian, whether brand new or experienced, to get comfortable in the confidence we have in our salvation. While Jesus has saved us from spiritual death, escaping Hell isn't our end goal by any means. Accepting Jesus' forgiveness is only the first step, essentially the doggie paddling, of living for Him. We must continue learning and growing, and the first lesson is that we will never learn all that God wants to teach us, and we will never arrive at perfection on this side of heaven. There is always more.

In order to continue to become like Christ, we need a community of believers that challenges and encourages us in our faith, we need to cling to hope, we need to serve those around us with love, and we need to confess our shortcomings. By realizing that we still have so much to learn, we make our hearts fertile soil for growth. Instead of explaining to God why we need no additional input or practice, we should always have an attitude that asks, "I wonder what new thing I'm going to learn next!"

Pray

Father, I am sorry for how I have stunted my growth by not acknowledging that I still have more to learn. Give me an attitude of readiness and excitement for what you want to show me next. When pride tempts me to ignore you, remind me of my need for continual training.

Reflect

In what way is God growing me right now?

Day Forty-Two

Decluttering

My third child was born in October. By the end of November, the amount of stuff in our house overwhelmed me. The combination of adding a family member and everyone being home all the time for the pandemic made me acutely aware of the constant clutter. Dishes, dirty laundry, toys, and half-finished craft projects constantly demanded my time and attention.

Ready to burn the house down in my postpartum exhaustion, I made a goal to get rid of fifty bags of stuff in one year. I ended up getting rid of over two hundred! Decluttering was a process. I started by carefully choosing things to get rid of. This shirt has a stain. These shoes are worn out. I didn't miss these things, and I celebrated one less item to wash, pick up and maintain with each choice. When I went through the house again, the question changed from "why should I part with this?" to "why should I keep this?" I have two whisks. Why? I have six infant bath towels. Do I really need all of them?

At this stage, I got rid of perfectly good items that were useful. In choosing to part with them, I made a conscious decision to value something other than having a full cabinet. In a world that demands that we always need more, and more is better, I can attest that for me, less has been such a breath of fresh air. I was drowning in things. Instead of me owning them, they owned me. There is so much more to life than keeping up with the stuff surrounding me. Can I truly love others well while spending so much time and energy on my belongings?

Read

No one can serve two masters. Either you will hate the one and love the other, or you will be devoted to the one and despise the other. You cannot serve both God and money. Therefore I tell you, do not worry about your life, what you will eat or drink; or about your body, what you will wear. Is not life more than food, and the body more than clothes?

Matthew 6:24-25, NIV

Apply

The same principle is true of the "stuff" in our hearts. What thoughts keep cycling through our minds, cluttering up our focus and distracting us from godly thoughts? What unhealthy habits and feelings do we refuse to let go of because we might need them one day? When we are trying to love others well, does our own brokenness keep us from being able to serve them effectively?

In order to serve Jesus wholeheartedly, we have to declutter our souls. We have to ask the tough questions about the things that we are holding on to: our reputation, our image, our secret failures, our dreams and goals, and our rights. While it is a challenge to let go of the things that we hold dear, they compete for God's throne in our heart, and there can only be one King there. Stripping away all the excess brings relief, freedom, and life!

Pray

Father, I am ready to take a hard look at the things cluttering my soul. Guide me in opening the embarrassing places, taking out the contents, and surrendering them to you. I want you to be the King of my heart, so strip away everything that completes with your will for my life. Give me a new life!

Reflect

What is competing for my attention that I need to let go of?

Day Forty-Three

Winning and Losing

Being all together every minute of every day for the summer can bring out the best and worst in our family. My very smart and sometimes sassy five-year-old has developed the habit of coming up with a reason or excuse for why she is exempt from obedience every single time I tell her to do something. This power struggle is exhausting. It steals the joy from our time together. It keeps us from being able to do certain activities in which obedience is necessary.

One night, after another battle of the wills, she comes to me in a rare moment of transparency. "Mom, when people argue with me, it makes me very sad."

"I feel the same way. Whenever I tell you to do something and you argue with me instead of being obedient, it makes me really sad, too. I don't enjoy arguing with you."

She looks at me skeptically, "No, you don't feel the same way that I do." The corners of her mouth turn down, and her voice wobbles, "It makes my eyes water, and it makes my throat feel hard."

It must be difficult for my daughter to believe that I, as the "winner" of every argument, could feel hurt by the exchange. How can the parent in charge feel like she is losing, too? Maya may not believe me, but yes, arguing with her makes me feel the same way.

Read

Oh, that their hearts would be inclined to fear me and keep all my commands always, so that it might go well with them and their children forever!

Deuteronomy 5:29, NIV

Apply

In the verse above, God is speaking to the ever rebellious Israelites. I love that I can feel the yearning in His words. I know how He feels. So much like my daughter, the Israelites excelled at finding any reason to disobey God's commands. When we argue with God, when we refuse to obey or endure with painful consequences, we get the idea that God is looking down, shaking his head and saying, "I told you so." This is so far from the truth. In this verse, God's heart is aching. He wants so badly for us to have the blessings that come from obedience.

God will win every time because He is God. One day, we will all bow a knee to Him, but today our refusal to obey is just as painful to Him as it is to us. Why? Because we are His children, and it damages the relationship that we share with Him. He loves us too much to allow us to wander away without consequences, and He mourns the loss of intimacy with us. When our hearts ache because God feels distant, He feels the same way that we do.

Pray

God, thank you for being a Father who desires to have an intimate relationship with me. Remind me that your commands are for my good, and obedience allows me to share in a wonderful adventure with you. Allow nothing to stand between me and obedience to you.

Reflect

How am I justifying my disobedience?

Day Forty-Four

The Boomerang Effect

You already know about my decluttering journey, and here is a pro tip: when you decide to part with an item, get rid of it immediately. I cleared out two shelves in the garage to house unwanted items until I can drop them at the nearest donation center. Putting things into the specified donation area keeps me from rummaging back through and pulling things out or second-guessing my decisions.

Eventually, this system broke down. While picking up the books in the nursery, I noticed one that I was sure I had put in the donation pile. And yet, here it was, back in the pile of books. Had I forgotten to put it in the donation area? I put it back in the donation pile.

The next day, the book was back, along with another baby toy that I had taken out earlier in the week. I put them back again, this time on the lookout for foul play. Sure enough, later that day, I heard a noise coming from the garage. My three-year-old was digging through the bags of donation items, her arms full of treasures to drag back into the house again.

Read

For as high as the heavens are above the earth, so great is his love for those who fear him; as far as the east is from the west, so far has he removed our transgressions from us.

Psalm 103:11-12, NIV

Apply

I refer to this mysterious reappearance of things that we thought we had gotten rid of as the "Boomerang Effect." Not only does it show up in our physical world, but also in our spiritual life. When we do something wrong, we confess our sin and ask for God's forgiveness. We put it behind us and move on with our lives in glorious freedom.

Days, weeks, or months later, something sparks a memory. We replay the scene of our fault on repeat, beating ourselves up more each time. We sink into shame like quicksand. The burden that we thought was gone is suddenly back, heavier than ever. How is this possible?

When Jesus forgives our sins, He doesn't simply decide to overlook them; He erases them completely. To Him, they are as far from us as the east is from the west. But Satan slinks out to the discard pile of forgiven sins and waves our faults in front of us, baiting us into unfounded self shame. When this happens, we must put the sin back in the trash where it belongs.

How can we keep from rehashing our sin? The answer is in verse eleven above. Instead of focusing on our sin, we ask God to remind us of His love, which is as high as the heavens are above the earth. No sin can separate us from His incredible love!

Pray

Father, thank you for your incredible love for me. Thank you for sending Jesus to take away the weight of my sin permanently. When I am tempted to drag up past mistakes and wallow in them, help me meditate on your great love for me instead.

Reflect

How has God's love changed me from who I used to be?

Day Forty-Five

Cross-Eyed Conundrum

My five-year-old learned how to cross her eyes this week. "Mom, am I doing it? I'm doing it! I can see two of you! Are my eyes pointing together in the middle?"

"Yes."

"Are they looking in the wrong direction of what they usually do?"

"Yes."

"I'm going to look in the mirror."

She dashes off to the mirror to make sure that I have accurately reported on her progress. Unfortunately, she quickly realizes that she cannot see herself with crossed eyes. She can cross them, but as soon as she tries to see herself performing her trick in the mirror, they straighten back out to view her own reflection. To make a long story short, much frustration ensued.

Read

[Jesus] asked [the disciples], "What were you arguing about on the road?" But they kept quiet because on the way they had argued about who was the greatest. Sitting down, Jesus called the Twelve and said, "Anyone who wants to be first must be the very last, and the servant of all."

Mark 9:33b-35, NIV (brackets added for context)

Apply

Like the disciples, when we follow God, we want to do it the best! But the best quality in a servant is humility, and humility is one of those tricky conundrums in the Bible. It goes against everything about how we think things should work.

In wanting to do good for God's kingdom, it is difficult to avoid a desire to be recognized for that same goodness. We learn to focus on others, to listen to God's prompting to reach out to the hurting, and then we notice we have done something incredible. Unfortunately, the moment we shift the focus back to how humble we have become, the virtue slips through our grasp.

Instead of reaching for humility in order to elevate our own reputation or status in the kingdom of God, we must change the focus entirely. We must serve God, looking to Him alone for our approval. When His glory is our end goal, we will serve in a way that helps others without seeking anything in return, even the gratitude of those we aid. Instead, we look into the face of Jesus and ask, "Have I given everything to follow you?"

"Yes."

"Have I brought you glory as a faithful servant?"

"Yes." The one least praised on earth is most honored in Heaven.

Pray

Father, help me stop trying to rate myself among your followers. When I am tempted to see how I measure up compared to others, bring me back to a place of humble service. Let me love you well by selflessly loving others, without recognition.

Reflect

Have I tried to rate my spirituality rather than focus on serving?

Day Forty-Six

Little Olympians

My girls love watching the Olympics. Let me set the scene for you: on the TV the best gymnasts in the world are completing impossible feats of agility and balance. On the rug in front of the TV are my wild-haired, energy-inflated toddlers.

"I can do that," one says, touching the floor with a foot in the air.

"Look at me, Mom!" says the other, front rolling into her sister, collapsing them both to the ground.

"Watch this!" the other interrupts, putting her head on the ground and flopping her legs onto the seat of the sofa.

It is, without a doubt, the most pathetic display of gymnastics I have ever seen in my life. However, at their age, they have more potential to become Olympians than I do. They have their entire lives ahead of them for training and growing. Most Olympic athletes learn their skill at a young age. My kids' Olympic dreams seem highly unlikely, but with the right training, they are possible. Never underestimate the power of a child completely devoted to a single goal.

Read

[Jesus'] divine power has given us everything we need for a godly life through our knowledge of him who called us by his own glory and goodness. Through these he has given us his very great and precious promises, so that through them you may participate in

the divine nature, having escaped the corruption in the world
caused by evil desires.

2 Peter 3:3-4, NIV

Apply

As Christians, we are training to follow Christ well. When we
open the Bible, we read stories of Jesus doing incredible things.
Like a child watching an athlete, we long to live like He lived, to
act as He acted, and speak as He spoke. We want our lives to
matter in the fight against the darkness in this world. However
impossible it seems for us to have the same influence as Christ, we
are downplaying our true abilities.

It is easy to believe that we are powerless to make a difference,
that our efforts for good are as unimpressive as my daughters'
laughable attempts at gymnastics. But that is not true. God has
given us everything we need to become Olympians for Christ. The
moment that we realize our full potential and begin training, we
wield the full power of the One who conquered sin and death.
Our actions can change the world. Our prayers can move
mountains. Our character can conquer evil.

We will make mistakes and fail miserably from time to time.
However, with a heart willing to learn and grow, we can tap into
our role as heirs to His promises and power. Never underestimate
the power of a life devoted to following Christ wholeheartedly.

Pray

Father, thank you for giving me everything I need to follow you
well and use your power for good. I resolve to be transformed by
your power so that I can use it for your glory and your good.

Reflect

In what way have I accepted the corruption of the world as
something that I am powerless to oppose?

Day Forty-Seven

Rock, Paper, Scissors

My daughter keeps asking me to play rock, paper, scissors with her. This is a simple enough request, but there is one problem. It requires two hands and my full attention. She asks to play while I am washing the dishes, folding the laundry, or changing a diaper. I keep telling her we will play later.

As I put off her request once again she says, "You know how you always say that we have to make time for important things? I don't think you want to make time for this."

Ouch. I'll admit that playing this game isn't at the top of my priority list over making dinner and giving the baby a bath. I tell her I want to play it with her just as soon as I have a moment to give her my full attention. The moment doesn't come.

In the last week of summer, I ask my daughter if there is anything else she wants to do before starting kindergarten. I want her to ask for something big, a fun outing, or a special treat. Instead, she wants to play rock, paper, scissors, and I did, with two hands and my full attention. I want to give my daughter the world: amazing vacations, lifelong memories, and unique experiences. Meanwhile, all she wants is five minutes of my full attention.

Read

[Martha] had a sister called Mary, who sat at the Lord's feet listening to what he said. But Martha was distracted by all the preparations that had to be made. She came to him and asked,

"Lord, don't you care that my sister has left me to do the work by myself? Tell her to help me!"

"Martha, Martha," the Lord answered, "you are worried and upset about many things, but few things are needed—or indeed only one. Mary has chosen what is better, and it will not be taken away from her."

Luke 10:39-42, NIV (brackets added for context)

Apply

The same is true of our relationship with God. As followers of Christ, we want to do big things for His kingdom. We want to take mission trips, lead others to know Him, and spearhead organizations and committees. These are good things, but we often neglect the best thing.

Above all else, God wants our full attention and both our hands. He wants us to take time daily to be with Him, reading His Word, talking to Him in prayer, and listening for His direction. Out of this simple, yet wholehearted practice, other requests may develop, but the foundation of a genuine relationship built over time must come first.

Why are we quick to do something challenging for God, yet we struggle to be faithful in the small, everyday act of spending time with Him? We want the trophy without going to practice. However, as any parent knows, the best moments are not the Disney vacations, but the simple games of rock, paper, scissors.

Pray

Father, I want to spend time with you. Help me develop a practice of being in your presence without an agenda. Help me value our time together more than any outward display of devotion.

Reflect

How can I prioritize my relationship with Christ today?

Day Forty-Eight

Shelter in Place

In South Louisiana, hurricane season is part of life. Everywhere the conversation is the same, "Are you evacuating or sticking it out?"

The answer is usually the same, "If it's a Category Three I'm staying, but if it gets to a Four or Five, I'm leaving."

We all watch the weather, attempt to predict the future, and try to discern the path of least disaster. If we choose to stay, we may regret being stuck at home without electricity or water for a week in the oppressive heat. If we choose to leave, we could get stuck in evacuation traffic for hours on the interstate.

We weigh the options and discern the decision with the least frustration. At some point, it is too late to decide. We have waited too long to leave and have no choice but to shelter in place.

Read

In your relationships with one another, have the same mindset as Christ Jesus: Who, being in very nature God, did not consider equality with God something to be used to his own advantage; rather, he made himself nothing by taking the very nature of a servant, being made in human likeness. And being found in appearance as a man, he humbled himself by becoming obedient to death— even death on a cross!

Philippians 2:5-8, NIV

The reason my Father loves me is that I lay down my life—only to take it up again. No one takes it from me, but I lay it down of my own accord. I have authority to lay it down and authority to take it up again. This command I received from my Father.

John 10:17-18, NIV

Apply

Jesus led His life with a different question in mind. He didn't ask what would be the path of least pain. He asked what course would result in the most love. I'm not talking about warm, fuzzy love, either, but the hard love that endures through adversity. He didn't come to earth with a "wait and see" attitude. Even though Jesus could have called off His decision to die on the cross, He resolved to fulfill His purpose.

As the eternal Son of God in heaven, Jesus had never experienced pain. He could have gotten to earth and decided this was more than He had bargained for. He had the power to "evacuate" at any moment.

Instead, He chose love. He chose us. He chose death. And now we get to choose. Will we pour our lives out for Him in return? Will we live our lives counting the cost of following Him and weighing the alternatives, or will we live unreservedly for the One who gave His all to save us?

Pray

Jesus, thank you for choosing to give your life for me when you could have turned back. Help me choose to love you and love others, even when it is gritty and hard. Give me the courage to follow you, no matter what risk that may incur.

Reflect

What do I risk by choosing to follow Jesus?

Day Forty-Nine

The Oak Tree

We have an enormous oak tree in our backyard. In the summer, its wide branches shelter us like a giant umbrella. I love this tree. Earlier this summer, I noticed a small hole in the trunk about eight feet from the ground. A few carpenter ants were traveling in and out of the hole, but I thought little of it.

Later I noticed another hole, this time at the root of the tree, with those same big black ants crawling in and out. I wondered if a tunnel connected the two holes inside the tree. Is it possible that this healthy oak tree could have a tunnel running the length of its trunk? Before hurricane season approached, we consulted a tree expert. He could only guess but advised that we remove the tree.

I reluctantly scheduled a crew to take down the tree and waited impatiently to see the extent of the damage. Had we acted too rashly? As the chainsaw ate through the wood, thousands of carpenter ants came pouring out like a waterfall, scattering in a frantic infestation. The tree was hollow. How long had this silent destruction taken place right under our noses? While it looked strong on the outside, the interior was rotted through.

Read

Not many of you should become teachers, my fellow believers, because you know that we who teach will be judged more strictly. We all stumble in many ways.

James 3:1-2b, NIV

Apply

How many times have we looked up to a Christian leader or friend, listened to their wisdom, and followed their leadership, only to discover later a silent sin rotting them from the inside out? We trust in their expertise like a child under the shade of a sturdy tree, without knowing that at any moment, a storm could blow them over with a great crash.

We have all had our faith betrayed by someone we admire, and it is devastating. While it is easy for us to shake our heads and wonder how such an oversight in faith could happen, we are vulnerable to the same fate. Our hearts are evil and bent on excusing ungodly behavior.

While some of us influence a few and others lead greater numbers, we all have others who are looking to us for direction, especially our own children. We have a responsibility to examine our lives, discover the areas of sin that need to be addressed, and deal with them.

When we see the signs, a little hole here and a few ants there, we can't ignore them. There is far too much at stake.

Pray

Father, you know how easily I can excuse behavior that is not right. Show me any area where I am saying one thing publicly and doing something else in my private life. Reveal the pockets of sin that are rotting my soul and give me the courage to deal with them quickly and completely, no matter the cost. I want to lead those around me without causing them to stumble because of my poor example.

Reflect

What unseen thoughts and attitudes need my attention?

Day Fifty

Unicorns

The internet solves a lot of disagreements in our house. My five-year-old seems to think that I know little about the world, especially compared to the World Wide Web. A very curious child, she has a lot of questions and rarely takes my word for it when I give an answer. For example:

"Mom, do unicorns exist in real life?" I shake my head. "But Lily says they do, just not on our planet. They live on other planets. Lily knows. She's eight!"

"That's not true. Do you think Lily knows more than me?"

"Let's ask the internet. OK, Google: Are unicorns real?"

Google: "I'm pretty sure I saw a unicorn once."

Maya bursts into a triumphant smile. Thanks a lot, Google. Just see if I don't unplug you for that little stunt.

Read

The law of the Lord is perfect, refreshing the soul. The statutes of the Lord are trustworthy, making wise the simple. The precepts of the Lord are right, giving joy to the heart. The commands of the Lord are radiant, giving light to the eyes. The fear of the Lord is pure, enduring forever. The decrees of the Lord are firm, and all of them are righteous. They are more precious than gold, than much pure gold; they are sweeter than honey, than honey from the honeycomb. By them your servant is warned; in keeping them there is great reward.

Psalm 19:7-11, NIV

Apply

In our world, there is a plethora of information coming at us all the time. It can be overwhelming. We can find answers, opinions, and even science to back up almost any idea that we want to be true. With all the conflicting facts and experts, it is difficult to navigate our way through making informed and wise decisions.

Or is it? Maybe we are looking for answers in the wrong places. We turn to our smartphones because, unlike the Bible, they will give us specific directions: eat this food, don't visit that vacation destination, exercise in this way, and don't wear clothes in these colors. However, after consulting the internet, I rarely feel at peace, filled with joy, or refreshed, as the verses above describe.

The Bible, while full of wisdom, is much more vague. It teaches us how to build a strong framework for making decisions. It drives us to pray, asking God to guide us in each step of our everyday lives. Our resulting choice will differ from mainstream thought, but we can have peace and assurance that it is the next right thing for us. When we have a problem, what is our first reaction? Do we have the urge to pick up our phone or to quiet our hearts before God?

Pray

Father, thank you for the Bible. What a precious gift that I have your own words to guide me in making decisions. Let me not become numb to the power of Scripture. As I search for truth from the Bible, give me peace, joy, and confidence in moving forward as you direct.

Reflect

What authority do I allow to define truth in my life?

Day Fifty-One

Faded Flowers

My three-year-old is at the age where she is understanding some Biblical ideas, but at a very basic level. For example, when I tell her that God made everything, she asks, "Then why did He make this road we are driving on so bumpy?" When I tell her He is in control of everything, she asks, "Then why does He make hurricanes and big storms come?"

As she looks at the world around her, she sees evidence of a God with quality control issues. The obvious brokenness of creation leaves her wondering how the God who created it could be good or have our best interests at heart. This week as we pulled up old plants from the garden, she said, "God is making all the plants die. I just don't know why."

Read

The Son is the image of the invisible God, the firstborn over all creation. For in him all things were created: things in heaven and on earth, visible and invisible, whether thrones or powers or rulers or authorities; all things have been created through him and for him. He is before all things, and in him all things hold together. [I present] the mystery that has been kept hidden for ages and generations, but is now disclosed to the Lord's people. To them God has chosen to make known among the Gentiles the glorious riches of this mystery, which is Christ in you, the hope of glory.
Colossians 1:15-17, 28-27, NIV (brackets added for context)

Apply

When things go wrong, we question why God's creation doesn't always reflect His goodness and perfection. In reality, God's original design was perfect. Our choice to sin ruined that perfection. As a result, the world is now condemned to suffer decay, death, and destruction but there's good news. Instead of leaving us to wallow in the consequences of our decisions, God sent Jesus to create a path of redemption, reconciling us to Himself.

The world is far from perfect, but we can discover two layers of hope amid the pain. The first layer is God's redemption at work today. There is life. There are miracles. God is still making things new, even in the surrounding darkness.

In the garden that day, I told my daughter that God is not making the plants die. He is the one that gives them life. Yes, the plant will face drought, storm, pestilence, and even death, but it will also produce seeds that sprout into new plants once again.

Our second layer of hope lies in our unspoiled inheritance in heaven. Because of Christ, we have true perfection to look forward to. We will one day see the creation God intended. We will experience life without pain, death, tears, or struggle, and we will worship our good God in all of His perfection.

Pray

Father, thank you for not giving up on me when I mess up. Thank you for sending Jesus to give me a second chance at being forgiven and called your child. When the world's brokenness weighs on my heart, remind me that this is not the end. Help me trust in your goodness as I wait for the day when you make all things new.

Reflect

How have I seen God's redemption in a broken world?

Day Fifty-Two

Learning to Snap

My eleven-month-old loves to mimic. She copies sounds, hand motions, and actions. This week while listening to music, I started snapping my fingers along with the song. Clara watched me in wonder at this unknown phenomenon. After a few moments of careful observation, she touched the tips of her finger to the tip of her thumb in time to the music, while clicking her tongue. I was so impressed with her ingenuity, putting the motion and sound together in her own way. While she thinks she is snapping, I know that her version is a clever imitation that resembles the real thing.

Read

It's like this: when I was a child I spoke and thought and reasoned as a child does. But when I became a man my thoughts grew far beyond those of my childhood, and now I have put away the childish things. In the same way, we can see and understand only a little about God now, as if we were peering at his reflection in a poor mirror; but someday we are going to see him in his completeness, face-to-face. Now all that I know is hazy and blurred, but then I will see everything clearly, just as clearly as God sees into my heart right now.

There are three things that remain—faith, hope, and love—and the greatest of these is love.

1 Corinthians 13:11-13, TLB

Apply

When we think about the mind and will of God, we often feel like my daughter. We watch God work with wide-eyed wonder, trying to figure out what He is up to and how He is accomplishing it. We try to imitate Him as best as we can, but our clever imitations fall short. We often react to this in one of two ways:

1) We decide that we have figured out how God works and announce it to the world. We expect everyone else to interpret God's intentions the same way. This leads to division.

2) We try to figure God out for a while, and after we see Him do inexplicable things, decide it's impossible. We hesitate to share our faith because we don't have all the answers. This leads to apathy.

The verses above show us how to live in the tension of not understanding God and living for Him anyway. This stance requires three ingredients: 1) Faith: belief that God is God and worthy of obedience even when we don't understand Him. 2) Hope: knowing that God is working things for good even when we can't see how. 3) Love: accepting that everyone will interpret God's intentions uniquely, and they are still His beloved creation.

Our imitation of God is blurry, but when we see Him in heaven, may it be with the words, "Well done, good and faithful servant!"

Pray

Father, show me how I have interpreted your will in a way that isn't accurate. Help me approach disagreements with others in humility, knowing that I cannot know you fully. When I want to give up, remind me that faith, hope, and love are the path to follow you. I can't wait to know you fully one day!

Reflect

How can I act with love, instead of superiority or resignation?

Day Fifty-Three

Team Spirit

My husband was watching a football game as my oldest daughter exercised her personal superpower to ask infinite questions.

"Which team is the United States?" she asked.

"Well, they are both from the United States. This isn't the Olympics. They play for different cities, not countries."

"Oh," she smiled contentedly, "so the United States will win either way."

"Um, yes."

"OK." And off she skipped to play with her dolls, no longer concerned about the game, winners or losers, or points on the scoreboard. She knew her team would win, no matter what. I love her perspective!

Read

So in Christ Jesus you are all children of God through faith, for all of you who were baptized into Christ have clothed yourselves with Christ. There is neither Jew nor Gentile, neither slave nor free, nor is there male and female, for you are all one in Christ Jesus. If you belong to Christ, then you are Abraham's seed, and heirs according to the promise.

Galatians 3:26-29, NIV

Apply

There are a lot of divisions in our world today: racial divisions, social divisions, and political divisions, just to name a few. The world teaches us to put on the colors of the team that we want to fight for. It encourages us to rage and battle and defend and conquer. We look at the scoreboard, and we square off against each other.

While we get caught in the weeds on so many differences that seem irreconcilable, we forget that God only makes one distinction when looking at a person. Does this individual belong to Jesus? Yes or no. There is no Republican or Democrat. There is no black or white. There is only team Jesus and everyone else.

When tempted to look at a fellow believer and draw lines of division, let's choose to put down our weapons and take up our cross. We don't want to be distracted by a detail, only to lose sight of the goal and begin attacking our own teammates. Just as my daughter saw two separate teams representing the same country, we can view each individual follower of Jesus as a beloved brother and sister. All followers of Christ have won eternal life and forgiveness from sin!

Pray

Father, thank you for inviting everyone to your kingdom. Instead of questioning others' worthiness, help me remember the grace you have given me. I am so undeserving of your love, and incredibly grateful for the gift of new life in Christ. May nothing else ever matter more to me than that.

Reflect

What divisions have I drawn in my heart and mind? How can I change my perspective?

Day Fifty-Four

The Locked Door

My three-year-old locked herself out of her room last week. While I have had my kids lock themselves *in* rooms several times, being locked *out* was a first. Everly turned the lock inside and then closed the bedroom door behind her on the way out.

When I asked her why she locked the door, she answered with her arms folded over her chest, "The only one allowed in my room is me."

"Well," I answered, "When you lock the door, it keeps everyone out, including you. Now you can't go in your room, either."

She didn't like that idea at all. I left it locked for several hours. She really missed having access to her room. When I finally unscrewed the doorknob to get it open again, I explained that the room would remain open to everyone, and she agreed.

Read

For if you forgive other people when they sin against you, your heavenly Father will also forgive you. But if you do not forgive others their sins, your Father will not forgive your sins.

Matthew 6:14-15, NIV

You received without paying; give without pay.

Matthew 10:8b, ESV

Apply

We seem to have a similar attitude to my daughter when it comes to forgiveness. When we make mistakes, we rest on the fact that God's forgiveness is complete and inexhaustible. What incredible grace that we can never "out-sin" God's ability to forgive and restore!

The issue enters when the tables turn, and others sin against us. Not being God, we aren't as eager to extend the same grace to those around us. What we quickly forget, though, is that forgiveness is an open door. It is an invitation to remain in a relationship with God, who is always waiting on the other side.

When we refuse to forgive those around us, we lock the door to God's grace. We create a barrier not only for others but also for ourselves. In denying grace to our neighbors, we are excluding ourselves from forgiveness as well.

It is an interesting double standard that we do nothing to earn or deserve God's forgiveness, and yet we feel that others should have to prove their worthiness in order to receive forgiveness from us. We cannot withhold what God gives us freely. And we cannot exclude others without excluding ourselves.

Pray

Father, when I am having trouble forgiving others, remind me of the depth to which you have forgiven me. Help me see the offender with your eyes. Give me the strength to extend the same grace that you do. Instead of allowing me to demand my rights, give me a heart of humility.

Reflect

Who do I need to forgive today?

Day Fifty-Five

Dancing Shoes

The challenge of decluttering is deciding what needs to go. A helpful question is, "Does this item reflect my current lifestyle, or a season I am no longer in?"

In my early twenties, I was a swing dance instructor, and during our dating period, my now-husband and I loved to cut a rug. With three kids under the age of five, we are in a different season. Our once-favorite dance spots open way past our bedtimes.

While cleaning out my closet, I had to face the fact that I owned several pairs of shoes and a bunch of dresses that were specific to an activity that I no longer took part in. While these items represent a season of life filled with wonderful memories, they no longer reflect who I am today. Swing dancing, while a part of who I was, is not a current hobby. I am enjoying different things now. It is time to let that piece of my life go.

Read

Each of you should use whatever gift you have received to serve others, as faithful stewards of God's grace in its various forms. If anyone speaks, they should do so as one who speaks the very words of God. If anyone serves, they should do so with the strength God provides, so that in all things God may be praised through Jesus Christ. To him be the glory and the power for ever and ever. Amen.

1 Peter 4:10-11, NIV

Apply

Seasonal changes occur in our spiritual journeys as well. How we serve God will shift in time as we follow His direction. In a season of caring for small children or an aging parent, our capacity for ministry outside the home may decrease, but our influence in the lives of those around us does not. We often believe the lie that what we used to do for God in another season was better. We compare our current work with the past and wonder if God is still pleased with our efforts. Serving in a quiet, low-profile position does not make us less important to God.

Our capacity for serving God fluctuates with each season, and so do the ways in which we serve. What does not change is our goal: to know Christ and make Him known. When we get caught up in doing, we forget we are called foremost to being. We must learn to detach our identity from accomplishments and focus on becoming who God wants us to be.

If we chase the feeling of significance that comes from prestigious ministry rather than serving for the glory of God, we miss the purpose of serving. When we let go of our glory from past achievements, we will serve as Jesus did, in the small and unseen ways. Instead of preaching to the masses, we focus on praying alone on the mountainside. Decluttering the trophies of kingdom work makes room for us to embody the hands and feet of Christ.

Pray

Father, thank you for the opportunity to be part of building your kingdom on earth. Help me find joy in serving you in whatever capacity you call me to in each season. Don't allow my past achievement to clutter the work you have given me today. Above all else, I want to know you and become like you.

Reflect

What past achievements or expectations are "cluttering" my soul?

Day Fifty-Six

Feeding the Ducks

My girls love to feed the ducks, and fall is my favorite time to do it. The cypress trees are bronzing, and their falling leaves create a soft red carpet over the grass. The girls break off pieces of bread and toss them into the water, where the ducks selfishly gobble them up and squabble with each other.

I spotted a neglected duck on the edge of the group and threw a few pieces of bread just to the left of him so he could get to them before the others. The duck completely ignored the bread and kept trying to fight the other ducks for the pieces in the middle. I threw some more pieces perfectly within reach, and he ignored them again.

After a few minutes, the duck turned to the side, and I noticed he was missing an eye. I threw a few pieces just to his other side, and he gobbled them right up. It wasn't that he didn't want the bread I had thrown, he simply couldn't see it on his blind side.

Read

For God so loved the world that he gave his one and only Son, that whoever believes in him shall not perish but have eternal life.

John 3:16 NIV

Apply

This verse is so well known that we often rush through it. Here is the humbling truth: God loved us, but we couldn't recognize His love. We needed something tangible instead of invisible. In order to see God, we first needed to know that God saw us.

So God sent His Son to earth, into our human world. He knew pain, loss, loneliness, and rejection. He felt all the extremes that we experience, even to the point of being killed by His own people while faultless. And yet, He loved with a love that this world is still reluctant to believe. He still loves us with that same unbelievable love, even on the days when we can't see it.

Sometimes when sharing my faith with others, they shut down, unable to relate to or recognize the love that I rely on with complete trust. While I toss out the breadcrumbs, hoping to draw them to the source of satisfaction, they don't gobble them up as I expect. Just like the duck at the pond, life has dealt them a blow that wounded them, blinding them to the truth. What can we do?

We must love like Jesus loved. We must love creatively, showing our love before we speak it. We must love unconditionally, loving each person as they are and where they are. And finally, we must love empowered by Christ. We must spend more time praying for this person in private than we ever spend preaching at them, asking God to give us wisdom and discernment to love them in a way that they can receive.

Pray

Jesus, help me love like you did: in person, up close and intimately. Give me your discernment to know how to love those around me so that they will trust you through my example. When I grow tired of trying, let your unconditional love fuel my confidence to keep loving others creatively.

Reflect

How can I *show* others I love them before I *tell* them that God loves them, too?

Day Fifty-Seven

Knowing You

At fourteen months old, Clara has spent almost every moment with me for over a year, and I believe I know her very well. I know which books she likes to read and which foods she likes to eat. However, since she cannot articulate her thoughts with words, there are a lot of things I can only assume. I believe she has a sweet personality because of her cute little smile, and I hope she is going to remain calm, sweet, and obedient.

I know better this time around though, because I have two other kids. Once they talk in sentences, their true personalities burst forth in full color. What I perceived in a single-dimension before takes on its full form and is never what I expected.

People are complex beings, with so many emotions, desires, needs, and expressions. There is no way that I can know my baby girl after only a year. I will continue to learn as long as she lives.

Read

I want to know Christ—yes, to know the power of his resurrection and participation in his sufferings, becoming like him in his death, and so, somehow, attaining to the resurrection from the dead.

Philippians 3:10-11a, NIV

Apply

This same idea of knowing can apply to our relationship with

Christ. There are many layers of getting to know Him. There is first what we hear about Him from other people, a vague idea that is tainted by their own perceptions. Then we read the Bible and see a better picture of who He is by examining His words and actions.

This limited perspective keeps Him between the pages, stuck in history. Once we spend time with Christ, letting Him speak into our current circumstances, we experience who He is in full color. We learn His promises and the truth about who we are, embracing our identity in Him.

Even this knowledge of Jesus reaches its limits, until life deals us a blow. Only in trials, challenges, and loss do we get to know Jesus at the most intimate level. When we drown in the overwhelming darkness of this broken world, we see His promises leap off of the pages of the Bible and carry us through.

When we know Jesus in our suffering, He is no longer an idea, a name, or a character from long ago. He is our Savior, our King, Provider, Prince of Peace, Sustainer, Fortress and hiding place, Redeemer, and Friend. When all else falls away and we ask, "Is Jesus all I need?", we can respond with a resounding "yes" because we know Jesus, and to know Him is to love Him above all else.

Pray

Jesus, I want to know you intimately. I give you permission to speak into my life, to lead me where you want me to go, and to use difficult circumstances to draw me closer to you. I desire above all else to know you and be known by you.

Reflect

How well do I know Jesus? Is it a personal relationship, or similar to knowing the character of a favorite book?

Day Fifty-Eight

All In

I grew up in South Louisiana near a river that ran through our neighborhood. Many of my childhood memories center on this one spot at the river that has a big hill and a giant oak tree. My friends and I would go there to have picnics, ride our bikes, play hide-and-seek, and explore nature. I spent more hours there than almost anywhere else.

A few years ago, I brought my girls there because I wanted to show them where I had played as a child. As we stood at the water's edge, a man came out of the house on the other side of the hill. A torrent of angry yelling ensued as he threatened to call the police if I didn't get away from his property. Apparently, a new owner had moved in and didn't appreciate a random person hanging around. It was sad to leave that special place that had always felt like home.

A few months ago, my sister and her husband bought an empty lot next to the neighbor who had yelled at us, wanting to build a house and raise their kids on the same river we grew up playing on. I warned her about this neighbor's explosive reaction, but when my sister met him, it was a different experience.

He told her that her kids were welcome to play in his backyard, along his section of the river, and in their hilltop tree house whenever they wanted. He explained, "A lot of strangers trespass in the area, but you live here. This is where you belong, and you are welcome anytime."

Read

Not everyone who says to me, 'Lord, Lord,' will enter the kingdom of heaven, but the one who does the will of my Father who is in heaven. On that day many will say to me, 'Lord, Lord, did we not prophesy in your name, and cast out demons in your name, and do many mighty works in your name?' And then will I declare to them, "I never knew you; depart from me, you workers of lawlessness."

Matthew 7:21-23, NIV

Apply

Many people grow up in the church. We spend a lot of time there, and it is familiar. However, the Bible clearly states that God will not admit into Heaven everyone who feels like a member. Proximity to God does not make us His children any more than playing on a property makes me its owner. While all are welcome, only those who take up residence truly belong.

In the same way that my sister and brother-in-law paid the money and signed the papers, we must lay down our lives and take up our cross to follow Jesus. We can hold nothing back but must move into a life dedicated to Him. Once we are all in, having sold our old house and committed to His mission, we become heirs of righteousness. While we can't earn His grace, we can choose whether to take the leap, get some skin in the game, and buy in.

Pray

Father, I don't want to be close to you without being all in. Show me any areas of my life in which I am holding back and not surrendering to you. Thank you for the promise that those who follow you will inherit your righteousness.

Reflect

Do I belong to Christ or just want to be accepted by association?

Day Fifty-Nine

Petty Party

"She is touching me with her feet, and I asked her to stop!"

"You didn't ask nicely! And you keep pulling the blanket to your side of the sofa!"

"Well, you knocked down the pillow fort I was building!"

"But you built it with my favorite pillow without permission!"

Bickering is one thing that can drain me as a parent. When my girls intentionally push each others' buttons all day, it is exhausting. I get tired of telling them to stop trying to frustrate one another. However, in every situation, there are two guilty parties. The first child wants to offend, but the second child wants to be offended. Once they retaliate, it creates a downward spiral in which no one wins.

Interestingly, when I split the girls up into their own rooms, they are disappointed that they don't get to play together any more. They fight for their rights, but their genuine desire is to have a friend to play with. They allow petty things to stand in their way.

Read

Like one who grabs a stray dog by the ears is someone who rushes into a quarrel not their own.

Proverbs 26:17, NIV

Apply

It is easy to identify our kids' pettiness but harder to see it in ourselves. We allow others to disintegrate our patience, peace, and joy, sometimes without even an actual in-person interaction. It can be a post on social media or a rule-breaking driver in traffic. It is tempting to allow these otherwise insignificant interactions to rile us up and make us defend our rights.

For example, a truck doing work on my neighbor's house has parked in the grass of my front yard for weeks, while my neighbor's yard is vehicle-free. My anger rises with each day, and I want to march over and demand that they move. But Jesus' still small voice tells me, "Step away from the petty." Ugh. I have every right to say something, but that is not the point. As soon as I value my personal vindication over a relationship, I am not showing love.

What can I accomplish with a confrontation? I would solve a temporary inconvenience and possibly do irreparable damage to my relationship with my new neighbor. What matters more? My grass or the kingdom of God? We can't let our fleeting frustrations keep us from God-sized work. If we keep our eyes on Jesus, we won't have time to be distracted by the petty.

Pray

Father, it is so difficult to not defend my rights over little things. Help me think of Jesus, who laid down His own life for crimes He did not commit to offer me forgiveness. Allow me to extend that same grace to others so that I can accomplish something of true value.

Reflect

In what situation do I need to step away from the petty today?

Day Sixty

Victor vs. Victim

A constant mom goal of mine is to keep the house tidy and plan meals better. Planning out chores and meals on my calendar has made a tremendous difference. The atmosphere in my home is much less stress-filled.

Before, I expected a constant mess with little kids gallivanting around, and for a long time I believed I couldn't do anything about it. Now, I still expect messes, but instead of throwing in the towel and letting everything look like a trash heap, I no longer let my home and my attitude become a victim of motherhood. Here is the truth: messes don't defeat my cleaning plan. They are the reason I have a plan in the first place!

Earlier this week I walked into the kitchen to find my fifteen-month-old so proud of herself for creating a sea of orange fish crackers in the kitchen. Instead of thinking, "this is the reason I don't clean," I smiled and grabbed the vacuum cleaner, thinking, "this is the reason I have a plan for cleaning". This is part of motherhood. This is going to happen. And then, I am going to clean it up. I choose to keep working at my goal.

Read

Dear friends, do not be surprised at the fiery ordeal that has come on you to test you, as though something strange were happening to you. But rejoice inasmuch as you participate in the sufferings of Christ, so that you may be overjoyed when his glory is revealed.

So then, those who suffer according to God's will should commit themselves to their faithful Creator and continue to do good.

1 Peter 4:12-13, 19, NIV

Apply

I have read this verse so many times, and I thought the message was pretty clear. There will be difficult times for those who follow Christ. Trials, loss, and suffering are par for the course, and shouldn't come as a surprise. So we just have to trudge through them.

While I was vacuuming up those crackers, though, I realized the significance of the second part of this passage. We don't have to throw our hands up in despair and become victims of suffering. Instead, Christ empowers us to take action.

Hard times come, and instead of succumbing to them, we make a choice to rejoice. We rejoice because we have the power of Christ within us. Yes, Jesus suffered terribly on earth, but He defeated death victoriously, and this hope is the source of joy. We will suffer as well, but we have victory waiting for us in Him. Suffering isn't a reason to lose our joy, it is the very reason that God has given us joy in the first place!

Pray

Father, thank you for sending Jesus as a tangible example of how to face trials in life. Thank you for not just telling me to "deal with it" but for empowering me to take action in the face of suffering. When I get overwhelmed by suffering, remind me that your joy is precisely for times like these.

Reflect

What am I allowing to steal my joy? What practical plan can I set in place to protect it?

Day Sixty-One

Meal Planning

Feeding five people three meals every day is exhausting. It consists scouring the internet for a new recipe that looks good, making sure that I have the ingredients, preparing the food while kids interrupt, and then cleaning up the disaster in the kitchen.

I proudly serve the food, only to have toddlers burst into tears for having to consume it. Repeat a few hours later for the next meal. I try really hard to please but always end up frustrated. I am haunted by the question, "What's for dinner?"

I recently started a meal plan that schedules out twelve weeks of recipes. Game. Changer. I don't have to figure out what to make, and I no longer pick meals to please others. I simply follow what is on the schedule. Since I didn't pick the meal, I have no personal feelings of rejection when my child fake gags through every bite. I am no longer a victim of dinner time shame.

Read

But Martha was distracted by all the preparations that had to be made. She came to him and asked, "Lord, don't you care that my sister has left me to do the work by myself? Tell her to help me!" "Martha, Martha," the Lord answered, "you are worried and upset about many things, but few things are needed—or indeed only one. Mary has chosen what is better, and it will not be taken away from her."

Luke 10:40-42, NIV

Apply

We can reach the same level of fatigue in our spiritual lives as we do with our everyday responsibilities. When needing direction from God, we scour the Bible for answers. We strive and stress and pray intensely. When the answer doesn't pop out immediately, we resort to trying really hard to accomplish big things for God as evidence that we are following His will.

Spiritual frustration originates when we shift from seeking God's will to trying to earn His approval by doing His will. We make the mistake of believing that following God's plan is a job to accomplish rather than a state of being. In the verses above, Martha thinks she knows what will make Jesus happy, and she is stressed about achieving that goal. Meanwhile, Mary is not worried about pleasing Jesus, but is finding satisfaction by being in His presence. The secret to doing God's will isn't in an award-winning performance but in a shared experience.

There is no need to impress God with a grand gesture. He just wants us. All of us. He wants us to love Him and delight in His presence. We no longer have to be haunted by the question, "What's next?" God doesn't want us to be victims of spiritual performance shame.

Pray

God, thank you for not being a boss to report my progress to, but a Father who wants to spend time with me. When I get anxious over what I need to accomplish for you, remind me that your will is to have my heart before my service. Show me how to delight in you.

Reflect

How can I shift my focus from doing to being?

Day Sixty-Two

Taste and See

When I got COVID, I temporarily lost my sense of smell and taste. I love flavor, and not being able to taste anything was so depressing. I first discovered my loss of taste when eating a grapefruit for breakfast. I took my first bite, expecting that beautiful balance of sweet and tangy that keeps me coming back for more. The cold, juicy texture was still there, but the taste was absent. It was like spooning squishy water into my mouth.

Later, when my daughter and I were snuggling together, I buried my nose in her warm baby hair. I took in a deep breath, expecting to inhale her usual scent of sweet innocence. Instead I smelled nothing. Just nothing. I didn't realize she had a scent until that devastating moment when it was gone. Eating food without taste or smell still provides my body with nutrients and energy to survive, but it lacks any vibrancy or pleasure. I took these two precious gifts for granted before, but not anymore.

Read

Follow God's example, therefore, as dearly loved children and walk in the way of love, just as Christ loved us and gave himself up for us as a fragrant offering and sacrifice to God.

Ephesians 5:1-2, NIV

Apply

Sin entered the world as a result of free will. Adam and Eve chose to disobey, which prompts the question, "Is free will worth it?"

Would God have been better off just creating a bunch of robots that obey Him? Life without free will is like life without smell and taste, a dull and meaningless march to death.

Christ came to give us abundant life, and that can't happen if we lack the ability to choose. Instead of compromising the incredible complexity of joy and pain that life can be, God chose instead to enter our mess.

Jesus shows us how to unlock the powerful possibilities free will can achieve for good. Jesus took all the evil that the world could muster. He shouldered it on the cross, and through love, conquered it, rising from the dead. We can do the same. When we imitate Christ and resolve to love others in the darkness of this world, we prove God right. The reward of choosing to follow Him far outweighs the apathy of a life without the ability to decide our loyalty.

And the best part of free will? Our sacrifice and worship are a pleasing aroma to God. When we obey, we give Him that deep breath of warm baby hair. We enter a shared space with God in which our proximity allows us to breathe in the same scent. Eating for sustenance pales to the chef's nuanced love of food. Choosing to sacrifice for God's glory transforms a mundane life into a beautiful, rich relationship with the divine Creator of the universe. What a priceless gift!

Pray

Father, thank you for the opportunity to choose you. Thank you for using every part of life, its beauty and its struggle to draw me closer to you. Allow my life to be a pleasing aroma to you.

Reflect

How can I enter a shared space with God today and show Christ's love to those around me?

Day Sixty-Three

Muddy Priorities

When tent camping with our girls, we had a beautiful spot on the edge of a lake. The girls explored while we pitched the tent. Within minutes, our middle child started yelling, stuck knee-deep in mud at the lake's edge.

Everly had trudged thirty feet out into the thickest mud I have ever seen. There was no way I could reach her without getting stuck, too. I pushed large branches out over the mud and walked on them like a balance beam, adding another branch to the end until I had fashioned a bridge of sorts until I reached her.

I grabbed her under the arms and pulled as hard as I could. With the suction sound of slurping mud, Everly's foot slipped out of her boot, completely buried in the mud. I lost my balance and managed a few steps along the branch before my foot missed and sunk deep into the muck. Wrestling my foot free, with my tennis shoe left behind, I struggled through the mud until we reached dry ground.

While Nathan took care of Everly, I braved the branches once more to retrieve the two lost shoes. Later, Nathan asked why I did that. In retrospect, saving the second-hand shoes was not worth risking the mud again. Why hadn't I just left them behind?

Read

If you try to hang on to your life, you will lose it. But if you give up your life for my sake, you will save it. And what do you benefit

if you gain the whole world but lose your own soul? Is anything
worth more than your soul?

Matthew 16:25-26, NLT

So you cannot become my disciple without giving up everything
you own.

Luke 14:33, NLT

Apply

The priorities we set in our spiritual lives can get muddy as well.
We look at those around us and make a list of necessary tasks to
achieve a full life. The list may include raising successful children,
gaining notoriety in a professional field, or getting attention on
social media.

I had to cross the mud to rescue my daughter, but going back to
get the shoes was unnecessary and unwise. It is the purpose of an
action that gives it value. In the same way, when our end goal is to
bring God glory, whatever we work at is worthwhile. It is not our
actions, but our purpose that gives our effort value.

When our purpose is to glorify ourselves, even our most noble
actions can only lead to meaninglessness. The most important
question we can ask ourselves as Christians is not what to do, but
why we do it. Let's not risk doing something great, only to find
that it accomplished nothing of value in eternity.

Pray

Father, thank you for giving me an eternal purpose. When I
consider what next step to take, help me spend just as much time
considering why I should take it. More than anything, I want my
life to bring you glory.

Reflect

What good action am I taking for a meaningless reason?

Day Sixty-Four

Compare and Contrast

My two older daughters' opposite personalities are easy to see at the dentist's office. Three-year-old Everly climbs into the chair without hesitation, lays down, and opens her mouth. When finished, she hops down with a smile to collect her prize.

My five-year-old, Maya, gets anxious the moment she sees the chair. She backs away, crying and hyperventilating. After all the persuasive techniques have failed, I take her in my lap and pin her arms under mine. She kicks, flails, and screams at the top of her lungs as the hygienist attempts to clean her teeth. She sounds like a wild animal being brutally murdered.

The shocked mother across from us probably left the office, concluding that one of my children was brave and the other was not. She is right. Everly is not afraid of the dentist at all.

While Everly set a great example, going to the dentist does not require her to be brave. While Maya experienced a first rate anxiety attack, it took more bravery for her to be forced into a cleaning than it did for Everly to be compliant.

Read

Jesus sat down opposite the place where the offerings were put and watched the crowd putting their money into the temple treasury. Many rich people threw in large amounts. But a poor widow came and put in two very small copper coins, worth only a few cents.

Calling his disciples to him, Jesus said, "Truly I tell you, this poor widow has put more into the treasury than all the others. They all gave out of their wealth; but she, out of her poverty, put in everything—all she had to live on."

Mark 12:41-44, NIV

Man looks on the outward appearance, but the Lord looks on the heart.

1 Samuel 16:7b, ESV

Apply

Comparison is a dangerous game for Christians because much of our progress is internal. It's easy to hold up our actions against others' and feel superior, while our spiritual well-being is lacking. There were many rich people at the temple that day with Jesus. Some gave large amounts and never felt the impact on their personal lives. But this woman, even though her gift was small, left the temple the most affected.

It may take the same amount of faith and surrender for one person to step through the doors of a church as it does for another to buy a one-way ticket to share the gospel in the jungles of New Guinea. God doesn't care about the extravagance of our gesture, but the sincerity of our hearts. God did not need the poor woman's two coins. He desired her devotion, and He wants ours as well.

Pray

Father, keep my eyes focused on you so that I don't fall into the trap of comparison. I want to do what you are calling me to without making myself less or greater in my own eyes by looking at others around me. I will follow you with all that I have.

Reflect

In which areas am I tempted to compare myself with others?

Day Sixty-Five

Attitude Adjustment

My oldest daughter is five going on fifteen, and on any given day I'm never sure which version of her I will face. One minute she is so sweet, creating thoughtful drawings and leaving them where I will find them or offering to help clean up around the house with a happy heart. The next minute, the eye rolling and sassy back talk come storming out like a volcanic explosion.

It probably doesn't help that we know how to push each others' buttons. When she obeys with a grudging and spiteful spirit, it sucks the life out of everyone around her. And when she skips happily to do the right thing with a smile, all is right with the world. It is her attitude, not her actions, that determine the atmosphere in our home.

Read

Therefore, my dear friends, as you have always obeyed—not only in my presence, but now much more in my absence—continue to work out your salvation with fear and trembling, for it is God who works in you to will and to act in order to fulfill his good purpose.

Philippians 2:12-13, NIV

You take no delight in sacrifices or offerings. I take joy in doing your will, my God, for your instructions are written on my heart.

Psalm 40:6a, 8, NLT

Apply

Especially in my role as a mother, I find it easy to do the right thing, such as cooking meals or cleaning messes, out of obligation or duty, but carry an attitude of victimhood or resentment with my work. This kind of obedience is not progress. A right action with a sour attitude is a silent poison. We must change our focus from doing the right thing to becoming the person who God created us to be.

When my baby wakes up crying for the tenth consecutive night, and I am so tired, I must change the internal narrative. I think, "I guess I'll get up again because that's what moms do." This attitude is deadly. We cannot tend to our child's needs from this vantage point, and it causes our own identity to deteriorate.

Instead, we can think of each action in terms of a piece of our soul transforming. When our child cries, we think, "I want to be a person who responds to the needs of those around me." Motivated by this goal, I get out of bed with a gentle spirit ready to meet my crying child with grace and patience. The difference is staggering. Instead of personal striving to meet expectation, this is the life-giving spirit of Christ at work in us.

Pray

Father, thank you for creating us as beings who have the potential to grow and learn and become someone increasingly like you. Help me correct my internal dialogue this week, so I stop trudging through the motions. Instead, help me rely on you to shape me through life's experiences. Let my right actions flow from a heart that is close to yours.

Reflect

How can I change my internal narrative from doing the right thing to becoming the person God created me to be?

Day Sixty-Six

Fruit Intake

Our family goes through a staggering amount of produce each week. My kids are mostly vegetarian by choice, and they will eat something green on their plate first every time. They will eat a whole cucumber for snack like it's a candy bar.

You might think that they get this love of fruits and vegetables from watching me eat them constantly. However, amid this fruit and vegetable-eating frenzy at my house, I recently noticed that my personal intake of these foods has plummeted. I am constantly rinsing, peeling, and slicing produce for the kids to snack on.

When I grab an apple for myself, I rarely get through cutting it up before a child swoops in and asks if they can have it. Before I can get another, I get interrupted and grab a granola bar instead. It is a strange truth. I love produce. I buy a lot of it. I prepare a lot of it. But I consume very little of it.

Read

Keep a close watch on how you live and on your teaching. Stay true to what is right for the sake of your own salvation and the salvation of those who hear you.

1 Timothy 4:16, NLT

You, then, who teach others, do you not teach yourself? You who preach against stealing, do you steal? You who say that people should not commit adultery, do you commit adultery? You who abhor idols, do you rob temples? You who boast in the law, do you dishonor God by breaking the law?

Romans 2:21-23, NIV

Apply

This trend in life doesn't stop with produce. We have constant access to God's Word. We have a Bible in every room, go to church each Sunday, teach the stories and principles to our children, and maybe even lead small groups or Bible studies. After being a Christian for some time, we inevitably end up handing out the truth we have learned. This is exactly how God designed it.

However, if we are not careful, we can fall into the habit of teaching and encouraging those around us but neglecting to spend time in God's Word for our own benefit. We are quick to share a verse on social media, but we don't allow that verse to sink into our hearts and press into the hidden places.

We mistakenly believe that spreading God's truth is the same as allowing it to infiltrate our souls. As long as we prioritize spiritually feeding others, we fail to nourish ourselves. Our focus must return to Christ for His own sake. As we become more like Him, the truth will flow from us naturally, without feeling like a duty.

Pray

Father, don't let me forget my first love for you. Instead of seeking the right way to share your truth, I want to sit and just soak it in.

Reflect

In what ways have I lost my personal practice of focusing on Christ?

Day Sixty-Seven

Peek-A-Boo

Experts say that playing peek-a-boo with babies is great for teaching the idea of object permanence. This is the concept that just because you cannot see something, it doesn't mean that it isn't there. If mom walks into the other room, she hasn't ceased to exist; she is simply in another place.

I guess I should have played more peek-a-boo with my older two because they still seem to have trouble grasping this idea. Cleaning up in the girls' rooms this week, I discovered granola bar wrappers stuffed under the bed, squeezed between the dresser and the wall, and tucked in their shoes. Busted!

Apparently, some unauthorized snacking has been happening. Hiding the wrappers doesn't make them disappear. The incriminating evidence is still there, even when it's out of sight.

Read

So we fix our eyes not on what is seen, but on what is unseen, since what is seen is temporary, but what is unseen is eternal.
                                                2 Corinthians 4:18, NIV

A good man brings good things out of the good stored up in his heart, and an evil man brings evil things out of the evil stored up in his heart. For the mouth speaks what the heart is full of.
                                                Luke 6:45, NIV

Apply

As adults, we understand the law of object permanence. Instead of simply covering up the evidence of our sinful actions, we learn to stop doing those actions. In our effort to be better, we can lose sight of what truly is permanent. While we spend most of our energy trying to clean up our actions, we often neglect the unseen attitudes of the heart. We don't steal, but we still harbor jealousy over what our neighbor has. We don't murder, but we still stew in our anger. We don't lie, but we still refuse to let the truth guide us.

We think we have gotten rid of the sin by changing the outward action, but our hearts give us away. The external self that we have spent so much time training to "be good" is temporary. Meanwhile, the internal attitudes in our heart are eternal. Following Christ isn't about cleaning up our deeds so we can *act* like Christ, it is about allowing Jesus to demolish us and recreate us into something new so that we can *be* like Christ.

It is a transformation of our identity first, which then flows naturally into external action. This is a slow, quiet, and painful work, but it is the only work that matters. The most permanent things that exist are the unseen qualities that Christ cultivates in our hearts.

Pray

Father, don't let me fall into the trap of behavior modification. When I am striving to do better, remind me I am incapable of permanent change on my own. I don't want to *act* differently. I want to *be* different. Search my heart and keep recreating it to reflect you.

Reflect

Am I trying to change my external behaviors or allowing God to recreate my heart?

Day Sixty-Eight

The True Prize

My daughter is in horseback riding lessons and just had her first horse show. I was so proud of her hard work. Maya's beaming smile proved she was proud of her accomplishment, and she went home with four ribbons, including a Reserve Champion.

The following week, she grabbed her highest award ribbon to bring to her lesson. When I asked why, she told me she had won four ribbons, but they didn't give any to Freckles, the horse, and she wanted to share. It was a sweet thought, but I suggested we give the horse one of her lesser ribbons or show it to him and bring it back home. Didn't she want to keep her first big prize?

She was adamant. At the stable, she hung the ribbon on Freckles' stall. In some ways, it seems like a waste, and in others, the highest prize possible. I was proud of her when she won the ribbon, but I was even more proud of her when she gave it away.

Read

Remember this: Whoever sows sparingly will also reap sparingly, and whoever sows generously will also reap generously. Each of you should give what you have decided in your heart to give, not reluctantly or under compulsion, for God loves a cheerful giver. This service that you perform is not only supplying the needs of the Lord's people but is also overflowing in many expressions of thanks to God.

2 Corinthians 9:6-7, 12, NIV

Apply

Many times, when we think about generosity, it's difficult to give to others because we believe people should receive only what they earn. When we work for something, we believe we deserve to keep it. When we recognize work worthy of payment, we pay accordingly. But knowing that something we give will go to waste makes it almost impossible to share freely. And yet, the Bible teaches us to give with a happy heart to those who haven't earned it and can't repay it.

Maya was more than happy to give away her best ribbon because she realized her dependence on her horse. Without Freckles, she wouldn't have earned any ribbons. A rider with no horse is useless. Yes, she put in the practice and worked hard to learn the skills, but she couldn't have done it without Freckles.

In the same way, we must shift our thinking in order to give generously. Without God, none of our efforts would be possible. God created everything we work to gain, including the mind and body that we use to achieve our goals. Yes, we work hard, but nothing is possible apart from Him. Therefore, it only makes sense to give God our very best. And if God tells us to give His share to those around us, we must do it. Sometimes this kind of generosity can seem like a waste, but the Bible teaches it is the greatest prize, because it expresses our gratitude to God.

Pray

Father, let me give generously to others, knowing that all I have is from you. Let my generosity reflect your love and not my opinion of who is deserving. Don't let me miss out on the true prize of demonstrating my gratitude to you, my greatest treasure.

Reflect

How have I given grudgingly or justified not giving to others?

Day Sixty-Nine

Pony Rides

This past weekend, we went to a sweet little spring festival with face painting, a petting zoo, pony rides, and bounce houses. The weather was beautiful, and the girls were ready for all the fun. First on the agenda was the pony ride. I prepped my oldest daughter, who rides horses, in advance.

"They won't let you ride on your own or go fast. They are going to hold the reins and walk the horse in a circle." I knew that the experience wouldn't meet her horseback riding capabilities.

When it was her turn, Maya jumped in the saddle and beamed a giant smile from beginning to end as the pony walked at sloth speed in a small circle. She was far from disappointed.

Read

Let the message of Christ dwell among you richly as you teach and admonish one another with all wisdom through psalms, hymns, and songs from the Spirit, singing to God with gratitude in your hearts. And whatever you do, whether in word or deed, do it all in the name of the Lord Jesus, giving thanks to God the Father through him.

Colossians 3: 16-17, NIV

[Jesus] put another parable before them, saying, "The kingdom of heaven is like a grain of mustard seed that a man took and sowed in his field. It is the smallest of all seeds, but when it has grown it is larger than all the garden plants and becomes a tree, so that the birds of the air come and make nests in its branches."

Matthew 13:31-32, ESV (brackets added for context)

Apply

Maya had joy riding the pony because she loves being on a horse, regardless of the circumstances. We can learn a lot from her in our own search for contentment. As we grow in faith and God gives us greater responsibilities, it's exciting to serve Him in "big" ways. The danger is that we can measure the value of our work by the impact that it has on others. Then, when we are called to work for the Lord in ways that are small, unseen, and unappreciated, we are reluctant. Those tasks don't have the same thrill or appeal.

In Colossians, we see that the value of our service and obedience has nothing to do with the impact or outward importance of our actions. Instead, the value lies in our relationship with Christ. The goal is to have Christ dwell among us richly. When we value that relationship over any accomplishment, we can have joy in every circumstance, whether walking in a circle on a pony or jumping in a competition ring.

Pray

Father, thank you for valuing a relationship with me more than you value anything that I could do for you. Help me remember to do whatever you place before me in joy, knowing that you are more than enough. I love you!

Reflect

In what area do I struggle with joy? How can I shift my focus to dwelling with Christ?

Day Seventy

The Eagle

Have you ever gotten upset with an author for killing off the main character? I guarantee the author has a more difficult time doing the deed than the reader has reading about it. The author, as the creator of that character, is more invested in their well-being than any outsider.

In my book, *The Enchanted Garden*, the Christ figure is a great golden eagle. In the original version of the story, the eagle's life was in grave danger, but he didn't die. I woke up one night with a terrible thought. The story is all wrong! The eagle has to die. I can't go 90% of the way and then skip the unpleasant part. Not only does he have to die, but as the author, I have to kill him.

Killing the eagle was so hard to do. Even though I know the happy end of the story, I cried. It hurt. I sat with the page forever, trying to find any other way to tell the story without doing the deed. Then I had to decide how it would happen. It couldn't be a peaceful death. As I typed the words, the tears flowed, and I hated myself for killing the eagle.

Read

Then Jesus went with his disciples to a place called Gethsemane, and he said to them, "Sit here while I go over there and pray." He took Peter and the two sons of Zebedee along with him, and he began to be sorrowful and troubled. Then he said to them, "My soul is overwhelmed with sorrow to the point of death. Stay here

and keep watch with me."
Going a little farther, he fell with his face to the ground and
prayed, "My Father, if it is possible, may this cup be taken from
me. Yet not as I will, but as you will."

Matthew 26:36-39, NIV

Apply

We consider how the Easter story affects us, forgetting the role
God had to play. God, the one who loves Jesus as part of Himself,
had to write the script. Together they knew what would happen,
and at 90% of the way, Jesus asked if there was any other path to
accomplish the desired end. Could it only come close to death?
No. Could it be a peaceful death? No.

We often believe that because the end of the story is victorious,
that the pain before it was not as difficult, but the suffering was
real. Jesus begs for any other option in the garden. He cries out in
anguish as His Father appears to forsake Him. The sense of loss is
overwhelming.

When the characters in my story see the eagle come back to life,
they run to embrace Him in joy and relief. We often forget the
deep relief, gratitude, and joy over the fact that Jesus is alive. But
He is! And it is a miracle.

Pray

Jesus, thank you for enduring so much pain for my sins. Thank you
for not turning back at the end, but finishing what you came to
do. I am sorry that your death was at my hands. Your love for me is
overwhelming. I love you!

Reflect

As I read the Easter story, which character do I relate the most?
Which one the least?

Day Seventy-One

The Linen Collar

This week I was moving a chest of drawers that my late grandmother had passed down to me. In order to move it, I took out all the drawers. Shoved behind the bottom drawer, was a linen dress collar, still in the packaging. When I opened it, the distinct fragrance of my grandmother's house enveloped me.

My grandmother loved having nice things, and she always bought the best of the best. This collar is no exception. The tag informed me it was hand-crafted at Presentation Convent in Cork, Ireland. How long has it sat forgotten, lost behind the drawer of the chest? It is sad that something so beautiful was never used.

Read

Then Mary took about a pint of pure nard, an expensive perfume; she poured it on Jesus' feet and wiped his feet with her hair. And the house was filled with the fragrance of the perfume.
 But one of his disciples, Judas Iscariot, who was later to betray him, objected, "Why wasn't this perfume sold and the money given to the poor? It was worth a year's wages." He did not say this because he cared about the poor but because he was a thief; as keeper of the money bag, he used to help himself to what was put into it.
"Leave her alone," Jesus replied. "It was intended that she should save this perfume for the day of my burial. You will always have the poor among you, but you will not always have me."

John 12:3-7, NIV

Apply

It is difficult to comprehend the gravity of Mary's actions in these verses. Can you imagine buying a diamond ring with your family's annual income and then tossing it into the ocean as a gift for God? Wouldn't it be better to donate that money to charity?

This story reveals two layers of regret we could experience in our lives. The first is that, like the collar, we have something of such value that we guard it and keep it safe, and it never gets used. We hoard our time and resources for ourselves. This is a waste.

The second regret is that we pour out all of our lives, our resources, and our energy in service to others, but we forget the reason it matters. This too is a waste.

We can fall into the same trap as Judas of being generous only when we see it will somehow benefit us. Do we give because we enjoy how it makes us feel? Do we serve because of the image we want to portray to others? Do we pour out our lives to earn God's affirmation?

Mary gives her very best, and she does it expecting nothing in return, even inciting the rebuke and disdain of those closest to Jesus. She gave completely, and she gave out of love for Jesus alone. This is never a waste. This is everything.

Pray

Father, allow me to give freely of my best, expecting nothing in return, knowing that all I have is from you. Help me find security in your promised love instead of striving to earn that love by my actions. Let me do everything out of love for you.

Reflect

What are the motivations behind my giving and serving?

Day Seventy-Two

Mom Fail

I picked up my middle daughter from Pre-K3 one Friday and began asking about her day. She told me that there was a party for the moms. Something clicked inside my brain. Oh, no! Today was Muffins with Mom and I missed it!

I pictured every kid in her class eating muffins with their mom. Then I imagined my daughter sitting alone, wondering why I wasn't there with her. I pulled the car over, looked in her eyes, and apologized. Then I took her to have a muffin picnic with me right then.

On the drive home, I wore sunglasses to hide my tears. I have felt that embarrassing loneliness, unsure of someone's love, and it hurts. I couldn't handle the intense grief of being the one who had inflicted that loneliness on someone I love. I was angry with myself for not being there. I hated the way my actions had made her feel. I would do anything to reverse time and be there.

Read

When Jesus arrived at Bethany, he was told that Lazarus had already been in his grave for four days. Martha said to Jesus, "Lord, if only you had been here, my brother would not have died. When Mary arrived and saw Jesus, she fell at his feet and said, "Lord, if only you had been here, my brother would not have died."
When Jesus saw her weeping and saw the other people wailing

with her, a deep anger welled up within him, and he was deeply troubled. "Where have you put him?" he asked them.
They told him, "Lord, come and see." Then Jesus wept. The people who were standing nearby said, "See how much he loved him!" Jesus was still angry as he arrived at the tomb, a cave with a stone rolled across its entrance. "Roll the stone aside," Jesus told them. Then Jesus shouted, "Lazarus, come out!" And the dead man came out, his hands and feet bound in graveclothes, his face wrapped in a headcloth. Jesus told them, "Unwrap him and let him go!"

John 11:17, 21, 32-35, 38-39, 43-44, NLT

Apply

Mary and Martha knew Jesus loved them, and yet, He wasn't there when they needed Him most. He showed up too late, and both sisters say the same thing: "if only you had been here…"

Yes, Jesus cried, but I had never noticed His anger. Two times the verses say Jesus was mad. Why? Unlike my anger at myself, Jesus was angry at death. This was never God's plan or design, and He is furious that we live in a world with pain and death.

Jesus set out to make things right. He raised Lazarus from the dead, but He didn't stop there. His entire purpose on earth was to set things right, not just for Lazarus, but for all of us. He would raise the dead again, but it would be the stone to his own grave rolling away the next time, and that resurrection would conquer the power of sin and death for all mankind.

Pray

Father, thank you for sending Jesus, not only to make things right again, but also to show your true heart in the flesh for us to see. When I feel alone, help me remember the depth of your love.

Reflect

How does Jesus' anger in this story help me understand His love?

Day Seventy-Three

Horse Swap

At six years old, Maya competed in her second horse show. When Maya entered the ring, her horse Freckles decided she did not want to compete that day. She started throwing her head forward, trying to pull my tiny girl right over the front. Then she started spinning in circles in place while trying to pull the reins from Maya's hands. Maya fought back, pulling hard on the reins and kicking with her heels.

But Freckles did not give up. She kept spinning until Maya was exhausted and frustrated from trying to stay in the saddle. Hot tears streamed down her face, but she did not stop fighting her horse.

At the end of the first round, Maya's coach ran into the ring with a new horse. She pulled a defeated Maya from Freckles and plopped her on to Ringo, as the judge gave the call for the second round to begin. With frustrated tears still streaming, Maya finished all three rounds. When the show was over, Maya gave Ringo a huge hug and didn't want to let go. She was so grateful that there had been a substitute, a wonderful replacement horse, to get her through the next two rounds.

Read

So I find this law at work: Although I want to do good, evil is right there with me. For in my inner being I delight in God's law; but I see another law at work in me, waging war against the law of my mind and making me a prisoner of the law of sin at work within me. What a wretched man I am! Who will rescue me from this body that is subject to death? Thanks be to God, who delivers me through Jesus Christ our Lord!

Romans 7: 21-25, NIV

Apply

We all know what it feels like to battle our sinful nature. Even though it is inside us, it seems like it has its own will, seeking to destroy us, derail us, and keep us from following God's instructions. We fight until we are exhausted and frustrated, but we know that this is a losing battle. We employ the advice my husband gives my girls all the time: "When things get hard, we try harder."

But we can never obey God by our sheer effort while perched on top of our sinful nature, no matter how much we despise it. It has its own desires, and it will not give up. Paul expresses our frustration perfectly. How wretched we are! Who will rescue us?

Do not lose hope! Right in the middle of our greatest need, God comes running into the ring with a new horse for us. He takes away our sinful nature and gives us a perfect substitute: Jesus. Thanks be to God! He sees our distress and finds a solution, a way out from the striving and struggling. We don't need to fight harder against our sinful nature; we need to swap horses. We must rely on Christ to get us through life's challenges.

Pray

Father, thank you for sending Jesus to rescue us from our sinful nature. When I am tempted to try harder and rely on my strength to do the right thing, remind me I can rest in you.

Reflect

In what areas of life am I trying hard instead of relying on Christ?

Day Seventy-Four

What Is the Goal?

After a year and a half of drastic decluttering, I am still at it, although at a slower pace. The most challenging part of this journey has been changing my philosophy about stuff. I am a frugal person, and my instinct is to get the monetary value out of something when getting rid of it. This would mean selling an item rather than donating it.

However, this thinking defeats the purpose of my goal. My goal for decluttering is not to make money, but to decrease the amount of possessions that need my attention. If I have to set up a garage sale in order to get rid of something, I have only caused more work for myself.

In order to reach my goal, I need to get rid of things as simply as possible, which means giving them away. While I haven't recouped the monetary value of these items, the unseen value of having less burden far outweighs it. Even so, it is a constant struggle. Each time I make a donation and the temptation to make a few dollars returns, I have to remind myself of the goal.

Read

But you are a chosen people, a royal priesthood, a holy nation, God's special possession, that you may declare the praises of him who called you out of darkness into his wonderful light.

1 Peter 2:9, NIV

Apply

Setting the goal for our lives can have the same clarifying effect. There are so many ways to spend our time and energy, and many of them are worthwhile. In order to keep our priorities straight, we must articulate the goal. That simple thought will sift every inner desire and keep us on the chosen path.

If our goal is perfection, then we will spend our time striving. If it is achievement, we will use our energy climbing the ladder. If it is comfort, we will use our resources to accumulate the best. If it is efficiency, we will value results over people. If it is appearance or reputation, we will seek others' approval.

It is far too easy to slip into a lifestyle that focuses on a goal that we didn't choose. And that goal will determine how we spend our time, energy, and resources, how we treat others, and what regrets will surface on our deathbeds. I am not here to tell you that there is one "right" goal, because the Bible proposes several meaningful options: making disciples, loving others, following Christ, and helping the poor, just to name a few.

Any of these goals, done to glorify God, will result in an unseen value that far outweighs any personal motivations we could have in life. I also know that it will go against everything inside of us to lay down our own agendas in order to advance God's. We will constantly have to refocus by asking, "What is the goal?"

Pray

Father, thank you for giving me a purpose beyond myself. Through you, I can invest my life in something greater, with an eternal purpose. Show me how to spend my time, energy, and resources to bring you glory. When I get distracted, remind me of the goal.

Reflect

What is the goal of my life?

Day Seventy-Five

Big Dreams

Soon my book *The Enchanted Garden* is going to have a version published in Ukrainian. Publishing a children's book in Ukrainian has never been on my bucket list, and yet, here we are! Like so many of the events in my life that have been the most meaningful, it came seemingly by accident. In reality, it was several small steps of obedience to a plan that I never could have dreamed up on my own.

My illustrator is a talented artist and inspiring Christian woman from Ukraine. The unexpected war in Ukraine changed everything for *The Enchanted Garden*. It pushed the publication back, but it also gave us time to consider how this project could bring hope for Ukrainian children.

We found a team of volunteer native Ukrainian speakers and began translating the text. This was far from the plan at the outset, and now it is one piece of the project that I am most excited to see come to completion. God works in mysterious ways!

Read

Now to him who is able to do immeasurably more than all we ask or imagine, according to his power that is at work within us, to him be glory in the church and in Christ Jesus throughout all generations, for ever and ever! Amen.

Ephesians 3:20-21, NIV

Apply

Moses was a fugitive from the law when God told him from a burning bush to lead the Israelites from slavery. Gideon was hiding from the enemy when God told him to lead an army against the Philistines. Ruth was a widow scrounging for food in a foreign land before she became the great-grandmother of King David. Mary was just a regular girl looking forward to her wedding day when she became pregnant with the Son of God.

None of these individuals planned or set goals to achieve any of these exceptional acts. They were simply going about life with a heart attentive to God. It is precisely their lack of ability to succeed on their own that allowed God to use them to do incredible things. They did not choose the adversity of their circumstances, but by following God's plan one small step at a time, they did far more than they ever could have imagined.

While the world encourages us to dream big and shoot for the stars, there are two problems with that mindset. 1) Our wildest goals can't touch the creativity of what God has in store. 2) When we set our energy towards building something great for ourselves, we are too busy to accept God's invitation to build something even greater for Him. God uses the unassuming followers who are obedient and those who stay faithful in dire circumstances to do amazing things that they never could have imagined.

Pray

Father, I want you to write my story. Don't let my own personal goals and dreams stop me from hearing your voice and following obediently wherever you want me to go. I surrender my future to you and ask you to use my time, talents, and resources to build your kingdom. Bring on the unexpected!

Reflect

In what ways has God worked in unimaginable ways in my life?

Day Seventy-Six

Nightmares

When I was little, I would occasionally have bad dreams, and I would creep down the hall to my parents' bedroom. I needed to feel my mom's comforting arms wrap around me and to hear her tell me that everything was going to be okay. There was one problem, though. My mom was asleep, and in order to get a hug, I would have to wake her up.

I would tiptoe into my parents' room and hover at the edge of the bed, staring at Mom's peaceful face, eyes closed, mouth slightly parted in the quiet, breathing in the even rhythm of sound slumber. I would stare at her intently, hoping that she would wake up at my mere presence. No such luck. I would whisper quietly, "Mom? Mom." Nothing.

I knew what I needed to do. I put out my small hand and touched her as gently as possible. My mom bolted upright in bed with an exaggerated gasp for air, as if she were dramatically surfacing from being waterboarded. Even though I knew this was coming because it happened every time, I would still jump in fear.

Once she was awake, my mother would give me the hug and reassurance I needed before tucking me into bed with a kiss. Whenever I was scared in the middle of the night, I always had to weigh in my mind if it was worth waking her up. Her sudden and frightening manner of waking up certainly set a threshold for me to decide how much I really needed her right then.

Read

I lift up my eyes to the hills—where does my help come from? My help comes from the LORD, the Maker of heaven and earth. He will not let your foot slip—he who watches over you will not slumber.

Psalm 121:1-3, NIV

Apply

Many times, when approaching God in times of fear or need, we relate Him to our parents. We weigh how much we need Him. We try to decide if our problem is worth bothering Him about. Depending on many varying factors, we set an internal threshold of need before we think it merits disrupting God.

Unlike our own parents, God is never doing something else that requires disrupting. He doesn't sleep, and He doesn't have a limited span of attention. He is always present for each of us, and He is always listening. It is difficult for us to fathom that the God of the Universe is constantly available to us, keeping us safe, and desiring to share in every moment. When we wake in the night, there is no need to tiptoe to another room to find Him. We have been wrapped in His loving arms the entire time. God is with us, and He is for us!

Pray

Father, thank you for being ever-present. Thank you for protecting me and not letting me slip. Remind me to go to you first when I have fears, not worrying about bothering you, but knowing that you are listening, no matter what.

Reflect

What is my threshold for bothering God? What have I tried to handle on my own this week that I can talk to Him about now?

Day Seventy-Seven

Swim Time

We swim after dinner almost every night in the summer. As we eat, we remind the girls to put on their swimsuits after the meal.

At twenty months old, Clara will stand up in her chair with both chubby arms stretched up over her head and shout, "Swim! Me! Me swim!" We assure her she will swim and convince her to sit down and finish her food.

As soon as we finish eating, the kids scatter. I clean off the table and check to see if the girls are ready. My six-year-old has wandered into the backyard and is picking flowers in the garden, singing to herself. My four-year-old is playing with dolls in her room. But Clara has opened her dresser drawer, found her swimsuit, taken off her clothes, and is now wearing one leg through the armhole and the other through the head hole, beaming with accomplishment. Amazed, I fix her swimsuit and try to get the other two girls to focus.

As I coax the others to get moving, Clara has pulled the swim bag from the closet. She distributes shoes and goggles to their owners. While the girls tire of hearing me tell them the same instructions a thousand times, they are much more responsive to Clara's adorable enthusiasm to help get them out the door.

Read

But in your hearts revere Christ as Lord. Always be prepared to give an answer to everyone who asks you to give the reason for the hope that you have. But do this with gentleness and respect, keeping a clear conscience, so that those who speak maliciously against your good behavior in Christ may be ashamed of their slander.

1 Peter 3:15-16, NIV

Apply

So many times I read this verse about being ready to give an answer, and I focus on the part about knowing what to say. When someone has a question about what I believe, will I know the right answer? What if I say the wrong words or don't know what to say at all?

I love how the verse tells us to have "an" answer rather than "the" answer. We can get so caught up in knowing what to say that we forget the other piece of instruction, which is how we should say it. We know that whatever our answer is, we must give it in gentleness and respect.

My girls are more likely to listen to Clara's two-word phrases chanted in eager excitement than my monotonous and long-winded instructions. In the same way, people are more willing to hear an imperfect answer spoken from genuine love than a correct one recited without conviction or care for the person listening.

Pray

Father, thank you for giving us Jesus, a great example of how to speak the truth in love, answering questions about faith with gentleness and respect. Help me to not only share the truth that I believe, but do it out of a genuine concern for others instead of a need to be right or heard.

Reflect

How can I show gentleness and respect while sharing what I believe?

Day Seventy-Eight

Raising Kittens

A stray cat took up residence under our backyard shed and gave birth to a litter of three kittens. The girls were ecstatic. They spent the next two months spoiling the kittens with snuggles, treats from their lunches, and elaborately created play areas until it was finally time to find new homes for their favorite furry friends.

When the new owners picked up the last kitten, my girls sobbed. It is hard to say goodbye to something that we love, especially when it is something to which we have invested our time and energy into. I told them I was proud of them for taking care of the kittens and making sure they were ready for their new families. Sometimes our work is for the benefit of someone else.

Read

"And Solomon, my son, learn to know the God of your ancestors intimately. Worship and serve him with your whole heart and a willing mind. For the Lord sees every heart and knows every plan and thought. If you seek him, you will find him. But if you forsake him, he will reject you forever. So take this seriously. The Lord has chosen you to build a Temple as his sanctuary. Be strong, and do the work."

1 Chronicles 28:9-10, NLT

Apply

A little backstory about the verses: David was the King of Israel and wanted to build a temple for God, but God told him his son,

Solomon, was the one for the job. David's response was to set his son up for success. He drew up construction plans, stockpiled supplies, and contracted workers. He put in the prep work and then handed this dream project over to someone else to complete.

We all know how it feels to let go of something that we have invested in. Our work on earth is to build up God's Kingdom, and many times that means doing hard work and not being the one to enjoy the fruit of that labor. It is challenging to trust that the next person will take care of our work as much as we do.

When the temptation to cling tightly to our ideas and achievements swells, we must remember we are not working for our own glory, but for God's. When it is time to pass the baton, we have several choices. We can refuse to give it up and put the future of the project at risk. We can let go reluctantly and bitterly, allowing our attitude to sour its future, or we can set the next leader up for success, regardless of who ends up with the credit.

While our culture is obsessed with recognition, let us be the ones who understand that the most important work happens behind the scenes. Success is determined by the choices that happen internally, led by motivations only God can see.

Pray

Father, thank you for allowing me to be part of the work that you are doing to build your Kingdom on earth. Help me remember that this is your work, and you care for it even more than I do. Search my motivations. Give me the desire to work hard and then gracefully release my hold when the time comes. May all the glory and credit go to you, always.

Reflect

When was the last time I let go of something precious to me? How did I respond?

Day Seventy-Nine

Metamorphosis

This summer the girls watched two kinds of creatures transform up close. The first were monarch butterflies. Our next-door neighbor sets out milkweed plants in the spring and tracks their progress. She invited my girls over to see the newly transformed butterflies and release them.

It amazed us how quickly the process advanced. From the time that the butterfly lays the eggs, it takes less than thirty days to become a fully formed butterfly, and the caterpillar is only in the chrysalis for a week. So much change happens so quickly!

The other creatures we watched were tadpoles. One morning, we discovered a long tube-like string of jelly in our little backyard pond dotted with thousands of tiny tadpole eggs. Within a week, there were swarms of tadpoles wriggling through the water. Slowly over weeks and months, the girls watched the tadpoles grow plump and round, silently sprouting little legs. It can take up to a full year for a tadpole to turn into a frog and hop away.

Read

So all of us who have had that veil removed can see and reflect the glory of the Lord. And the Lord—who is the Spirit—makes us more and more like him as we are changed into his glorious image.

2 Corinthians 3:18, NLT

Apply

As Christ's followers, we can relate to butterflies. We have experienced the immediate transformation of being forgiven by Christ. Considering that change, it is discouraging when our thoughts, words, and actions don't reflect the metamorphosis of our hearts. We forget an important truth: there are two transformations that happen in our walk with Jesus.

The first is being forgiven of our sin, a change as striking and speedy as a caterpillar becoming a butterfly. Unlike a monarch, salvation does not mean arriving at our final state but rather restarting at a new beginning. We hatch out of our chrysalis to find we are tadpole eggs, with a long journey of slow maturing ahead.

This second stage of development is lifelong, moving forward imperceptibly, as we learn to rely on God, obey His Word, and follow Him moment by moment. Often we look back in surprise and wonder: When did I start trusting God with my fears instead of trying to control? When did I begin responding with a gentle answer instead of impatience? When did I start longing for time in God's Word more than other distractions?

The Christian life is two metamorphoses: the first fast and miraculous, and the second slow and gradually deepening. What a beautiful creature God has in mind for us to become!

Pray

Father, thank you for Jesus' sacrifice on the cross that allows me to become a new creation. When I am frustrated by recurring sin, encourage me knowing that I am still growing deeper, and that you are not finished with me yet.

Reflect

In what ways have I changed to become more like Christ? In what areas is God still working on me? How have I responded?

Day Eighty

Cast On, Cast Off

My twenty-one-month-old broke her leg at a trampoline park. For the next three weeks, she wore a heavy cast from her tiny toes up to her chunky thigh. The first day with the cast, she was so frustrated at her immobility. She could sit up, and that was the extent of her movement. She wanted that cast off so she could run around with her sisters again.

By the next day, she was sliding herself across the floor on her belly in a zombie style. By the third day, she was pulling up to a standing position on furniture, and by day four with a cast, she took her first tentative steps across the room, lugging that bulky mass along with her.

She is very independent, and her favorite phrase when I try to help is, "I got it." I can only imagine what activities she will hobble through in another two and a half weeks. She may forget the freedom of effortless movement before the cast.

Read

Therefore, since we are surrounded by such a great cloud of witnesses, let us throw off everything that hinders and the sin that so easily entangles. And let us run with perseverance the race marked out for us, fixing our eyes on Jesus, the pioneer and perfecter of faith.

Hebrews 12:1-2a, NIV

Apply

Humans have an incredible capacity for resilience and adaptability. It is our strength and our weakness. When something in life threatens to slow us down, we innovate and power through. We cling to our independence and say, "I got it."

Unfortunately, some of what we learn to live with should actually be cast off (pun intended). We layer on minor sins, allowing them to stay with us as we make justifications for why they aren't so bad. They collect and weigh us down. They limit our ability to move and muffle God's voice. We are so proud of what we can accomplish despite our entanglements that we forget what freedom feels like.

My daughter may have figured out how to move with a giant cast on her leg, but she can't run a race with it on. It must come off, and the sooner the better, in order for her to regain full mobility.

It is the same with the sins in our lives, whether we label them big or small. Criticism, comparison, gossip, pride, and pettiness handicap us in our race. They distract our focus from Christ and distort our view of what is important. If we are serious about running for Christ, everything that slows us down has to go.

Pray

Father, I am sorry for how I have made excuses for the sin in my life. I'm sorry for the energy that I have wasted trying to make life work without having to leave that sin behind. Show me what I need to cast aside in order to follow you wholeheartedly, and give me the discipline to do the hard work of following through. Thank you for the freedom you offer and for giving me the strength to choose you.

Reflect

What sin do I need to cast off this week?

Day Eighty-One

No Words

Can I confess having an unpopular opinion? I don't like babies. They are nice, but I am not a "baby person." I love kids and have spent most of my life working with kids, but the baby phase has never been my jam.

I like when kids are old enough to talk, to tell me what they need and want, and to have a meaningful conversation with me. As a person whose love language is words, I feel powerless trying to establish a relationship with a tiny person who can't speak yet.

When I was pregnant with my eldest, I was so excited. I have always wanted to be a mom, and I couldn't wait to have kids, but I was hesitant about surviving the baby phase to get there. But then something unexpected happened: I met my baby.

The beginning was rough, but spending so much time with one tiny crying human meant we built a relationship based on something other than words. It was instinctual. It was a mix of smells and cuddles and intuition and empathy that created an unspoken understanding between the two of us.

I was her mother, and I knew her better than anyone else in the world. I could read her mind, her moods, and her meaning long before she could tell me anything with words. Not only did I know her completely, but I could also help others to know her by explaining why she was upset, how to calm her, and what she liked.

Read

In the same way, the Spirit helps us in our weakness. We do not know what we ought to pray for, but the Spirit himself intercedes for us through wordless groans. And he who searches our hearts knows the mind of the Spirit, because the Spirit intercedes for God's people in accordance with the will of God.

Romans 8:26-27, NIV

Apply

When praying, we often feel the need to find the right words, as if incorrect or unclear wording will cause God to misunderstand our requests or intentions. We forget God is our Father, and He made us. He knows us better than anyone else. Long before we could use words, He knew our thoughts and desires.

While words may be helpful for us in figuring out our needs, they are unnecessary for Him. We also have the Spirit to help us when we don't have the words. He interprets our groaning to the Father on our behalf.

When our pain is too unbearable for words, He sits silently beside us, collecting our tears, with no explanation necessary. When the joy is complicated and mixes with loss, He understands. These layers of emotions aren't too complicated for Him. He knows our needs; He knows our heart, and His presence is enough.

Pray

Father, thank you for knowing me better than I know myself. Help me trust you when the words fail. Let me not give up on spending time with you, but refill my soul by simply being in your presence.

Reflect

Spend a few minutes sitting with the Father in silence.

Day Eighty-Two

Zinnias

Zinnias are one of my favorite flowers. I grow them every year in my garden, and many times they grow back on their own, reseeding naturally from the previous year's plants. My favorite heirloom variety grows over three feet tall. By late summer, the plants are towering and long past their spring prime. The long stems droop under the weight of the plant. The leaves are yellow and covered in brown spots, wilting in the summer heat. They are so overgrown that I am tempted to pull them all up.

And yet, each time I reach to uproot them, I am stopped short by the joyful burst of color of these cheerful flowers. Even though the stems and leaves are suffering from the unrelenting heat of summer, the flowers are flawless. The blossoms are full and bright, perfect circles of aligned petals in flashes of pink, orange, and red. If I yank them out now, these plants will lose their ability to deposit the seeds for next year's dazzling array of blooms.

Read

I consider that our present sufferings are not worth comparing with the glory that will be revealed in us. For the creation waits in eager expectation for the children of God to be revealed. For the creation was subjected to frustration, not by its own choice, but by the will of the one who subjected it, in hope that the creation itself will be liberated from its bondage to decay and brought into the freedom and glory of the children of God.
We know that the whole creation has been groaning as in the pains

of childbirth right up to the present time. Not only so, but we ourselves, who have the firstfruits of the Spirit, groan inwardly as we wait eagerly for our adoption to sonship, the redemption of our bodies. For in this hope we were saved.

Romans 8:18-24a, NIV

Apply

Sometimes there is a part of our lives that isn't growing how we had in mind. We survey the crooked stem of expectations, the leaves spotted with disappointment and failure, and wonder if it is time to uproot the entire dream and move on. Especially in seasons when we have been sweltering in oppressive heat, we forget that the purpose of our lives is to reseed.

Reseeding requires each flower to lay down its petals and surrender to the soil, but it first requires the flowers to bloom. Without a vibrant flower of hope and faith amid the glaring sun and pounding rain, there can be no fertilization. Without a beauty that draws the bees and butterflies to its fruitful center, the seeds remain unable to reproduce.

In the same way, the beauty of our hope in God draws others to the display of His unfailing love in our lives, even when our strength is faltering. Only then can we achieve our true purpose, not to be strong, but to surrender, so that when our lives eventually fade away, we leave behind a garden littered with fertile seed to sprout for another generation.

Pray

Father, thank you for using even the hard seasons of life for a beautiful purpose. Help me remember that seasons of growth and seasons of release are all to bring you glory.

Reflect

What kind of season am I in right now? How can I serve God in it?

Day Eighty-Three

Gaining Confidence

When my twenty-one-month-old got her cast off of her broken leg, I expected her to take off running in every direction in newfound freedom. That was far from reality. She got it off in the morning and didn't move on her own at all that day. No crawling or even scooting. She was very tentative about using her newly-healed leg.

That night we went swimming for the first time in a month because she could finally get her leg wet again. I put Clara in her puddle jumper and let her float around. In the water, she felt comfortable moving her leg, bending the knee, and kicking around. Her confidence grew, and when it was time to get out of the pool, she walked up the steps on her own and stood on dry ground with confidence.

Even a week later, she is still hobbling around like a pirate with a peg leg, stiff and unsteady. The doctor reminds us it will take practice to strengthen the muscles that were unused for so long and give her the confidence to grow in ability. In fact, a broken bone that heals completely is stronger than the bone was before it broke, even if it doesn't seem that way at first.

Read

In him and through faith in him we may approach God with freedom and confidence.

Ephesians 3:12, NIV

Apply

Sometimes in our walk with God, we experience setbacks. These broken bones in our faith can result from the loss of someone we love, the failure of someone we look up to, or the grief and suffering that comes with life. We know that God, as the Healer, can bind up our broken hearts and help us through these seasons, but on the other side, it's difficult to regain the same confidence we had before in our relationship with Him.

This unsteadiness stems not from a lack of ability but from a lack of practice. Our faith is a muscle, and our relationship with Him can grow or shrink with the amount that we exercise it. When we trust in God in moments when it makes little sense, when all rational thought would urge us to take matters into our own hands or at least demand that He act on our behalf, it is like stretching our muscles in the swimming pool of faith.

When God shows up and creates the most unexpected and beautiful redemption from our pain, our confidence grows. This cycle of trusting in moments of uncertainty and recognizing God's faithful protection and provision is vital to approaching God with freedom and confidence. A faith that is tested, broken, and then reaffirmed is stronger than one that has never faced adversity.

Pray

Father, thank you for being unchanging. Thank you for promising to provide for me, to have good plans for me, and to guide me as I follow you. Give me a strong faith: one that relies on you even when your plan is impossible to discern. Grow my faith so that I can come to you with freedom and confidence.

Reflect

How has God worked amid trials in my life?

Day Eighty-Four

DIY Disaster

My girls love crafting, especially with perler beads. The girls set the tiny plastic beads one at a time on a pegboard base and make different designs. When they finish the creation, we melt the beads together with an iron, setting the design into its permanent state.

There is one minor problem with this craft, and that is the fact that it takes several days for the girls to finish their designs. In the meantime, the beads sit on their pegboards on the counter. Amid the daily bustle, the pegboards get bumped, and the little beads fall off of their pegs and go rolling across the counter.

The meticulous designs get destroyed repeatedly. The girls make some progress until the next day, when they have to rework the same section yet again. The never-ending task of replacing disrupted beads continues. They finally ask for my help to get the job done, and then we can all move on to the next project.

Read

For God, who said, "Let light shine out of darkness," made his light shine in our hearts to give us the light of the knowledge of God's glory displayed in the face of Christ. But we have this treasure in jars of clay to show that this all-surpassing power is from God and not from us. We are hard pressed on every side, but not crushed; perplexed, but not in despair; persecuted, but not abandoned; struck down, but not destroyed.

2 Corinthians 4:6-9, NIV

Apply

Do you ever feel you are playing catch up? Just when you think you are getting your feet back under you, something in life disrupts the perfectly placed pieces, and you rush to put them all back yet again. If only we could get everything the way we want it and then freeze it right there! But we know this isn't how life really works.

In the verses above, Paul explains that we have God's glory shining in our hearts. As followers of Christ, we have assurance that we are His. Our salvation is fused together and cannot be broken. But... do you see the "but" at the beginning of the next sentence? We have this permanent place in Christ housed in a very fragile receptacle. It doesn't take much to bump our peg boards and send all the beads rolling.

And yet, while our messiness is far from our design, it is God's design. He places His glory in our weakness to display His power. The uncertainty of our lives pushes us to depend on Him, to turn to Him in our moments of weakness, and to shine His light for those around us. And when we rely on His strength, nothing can crush us. The pieces will fall apart, but they will never be beyond repair, and instead of frantically trying to fix the board on our own, God will fill us with His peace and patience as we faithfully work together on one bead at a time.

Pray

Father, thank you that I am not alone in this life. Thank you for your light that shines through me despite my weaknesses. Give me the wisdom to rely on you in every situation. Instead of trying to fix my life myself, I will ask for your help and direction.

Reflect

In what area of my life am I trying to fix the pieces on my own?

Day Eighty-Five

Diapers on Duty

WARNING: This devotion includes bodily fluids. If you are sensitive to that, skip it. I've included it because bodily fluids are part of mom life.

I have changed five to fifteen diapers every day for the last six years. But one day, I will be done with diapers. One glorious day, hopefully soon, my last kid will finish potty training, and my diaper changing years will be over. Clara is starting to potty train, and when she uses the big girl potty, I do a happy dance and cheer and shower her with fruit snacks! This is something to celebrate!

Don't get me wrong, I am thankful for diapers. Having something that keeps all the fluids and solids from getting all over everything is very helpful. They serve an important purpose for a season, but they aren't a long-term solution. Babies may not see the problems with diapers, but parents do. It is really messy to have to deal with another person's waste multiple times a day.

The biggest problem: diapers don't make the poo disappear, they just hold it. Toilets flush it away like it was never there. That is the long-term solution! My daughters will never stop using the bathroom, but I welcome the day that they all do it in the toilet.

Read

Day after day every priest stands and performs his religious duties; again and again he offers the same sacrifices, which can never take away sins. But when this priest [Jesus] had offered for all time one sacrifice for sins, he sat down at the right hand of

God. For by one sacrifice he has made perfect forever those who are being made holy.

Hebrews 10:11-12, 14, NIV (brackets added for context)

Apply

It is difficult as modern Christians to understand the full significance of Jesus' death and resurrection because we don't remember the "before" part of the story. In the Old Testament, the Jews had a temporary way to deal with sin, and that was the sacrificial system.

The punishment for sin is death, so priests would sacrifice animals to pay the price for the people's sin. However, there were some drawbacks to the system. It was a temporary fix that had to be repeated every time they committed another sin. It also didn't take the sins away: it just covered them up for a while until they could find a permanent solution.

Then Jesus enters the scene. For lack of a more elegant analogy, Jesus shows up with a toilet that flushes sins away completely. We will never stop sinning as long as we live, but through Christ, we have a way to deal with sin that is permanent. He brought the long-term solution that we needed. No more sacrifices, tallying, or keeping score. Our sin is gone! That is something to celebrate!

Pray

Father, thank you for sending Jesus as a permanent solution for my sin. Thank you for not keeping track of what I do wrong, but for seeing Jesus' perfection in my place. I am so grateful for and unworthy of your incredible love!

Reflect

What is something I have done and am still carrying around? Can I mentally put it in the toilet and watch it swirl away?

Day Eighty-Six

The Greatest Adventure

My husband and I spent a week at St. Thomas in the Virgin Islands. It was the trip of a lifetime. The white sand beaches and crystal clear water were amazing. We experienced some amazing adventures, including scuba diving with spotted eagle rays, kayaking in mangrove forests, snorkeling in coral reefs, and my favorite, swimming eye to eye with six-foot sea turtles off the coast of St. John. These experiences were unbelievable bucket list activities we may never take part in again.

And yet, at the end of our trip, I couldn't wait to get back home. What about south Louisiana could have me ready to leave such an incredible paradise? I'll give you a hint: it is something that isn't anywhere else. Back in our hometown, we drive up the familiar street, pull into the garage piled with pink bikes, and open our door that sticks on that one tile. We creep to the bedrooms and gaze at three beautiful little sleeping faces. Our actions in these four walls determine our legacy.

These three girls are the greatest adventure. My first day back with them included bubbles, bike rides, blocks, and books. We splashed in puddles on the sidewalk and pulled weeds in the garden. We snuggled and tickled and crafted.

It's true that none of these activities are bucket-list-worthy, but this experience, this season with my kids, is priceless. I could search the entire world and not find anything more valuable than these simple moments.

Read

The Lord your God is in your midst, a mighty one who will save; he will rejoice over you with gladness; he will quiet you by his love; he will exult over you with loud singing.

Zephaniah 3:17, ESV

Apply

Did you know God feels the same way about us: a parent who cherishes time with His children? God, the Creator of the universe, the One who hung the stars and invented the creatures in the deepest ocean, can't wait to spend time with you. In all the cosmos, His attention is on us. We are His greatest creation, His favorite adventure, His precious children. He looks down at our sleeping faces and longs for the moment when we open our eyes because He wants to spend time with us.

He loved us so much that Jesus left the paradise of heaven to enter our world and create a way for us to be called the Father's children. He waits expectantly for us to open His Word, sit in silence in His presence, and be with Him. What He has done for us is His eternal legacy, His undeserved declaration of love. And how we respond to that incredible love is the greatest adventure of our lives!

Pray

Father, thank you for loving me as a parent loves a child. Of everything in existence, you took special notice of me and gave your own Son's life for mine. I can never deserve your love and yet you give it to me freely. Help me set my eyes on you as the most important object of pursuit.

Reflect

How will I respond to God's declaration of love today?

Day Eighty-Seven

Scuba Diving

On our vacation my husband and I went scuba diving. First we had a class, then our group headed to the beach with the instructor, where we tested our skills in four feet of water.

My first breath from the regulator sounded like a monster growl. I tried to breathe normally like we learned, but my brain jumped into survival mode. It said, "Stop! You can't breathe underwater! Surface and save yourself!" I panicked and popped out of the water. I was freaking out, wondering if I could follow through with the dive at all.

"It's normal," the instructor above the water commented on my panic. "People weren't born with gills. Try again."

I forced myself to put my head back in the water and take a breath. The next few minutes were a mental battle in which I had to fight every urge to surface. I convinced myself that breathing underwater was totally fine. We practiced the skills we had rehearsed in class, and then spent the next hour exploring coral reefs, tropical fish, and aquatic creatures forty feet down. I am so glad I pushed past the mental block I experience at four feet below the surface.

Read

"Lord, if it's you," Peter replied, "tell me to come to you on the water."
"Come," he said.

Then Peter got down out of the boat, walked on the water and came toward Jesus. But when he saw the wind, he was afraid and, beginning to sink, cried out, "Lord, save me!"
Immediately Jesus reached out his hand and caught him. "You of little faith," he said, "why did you doubt?"

Matthew 14:29-31, NIV

Apply

We know God has power over everything in the universe, but we live within the constraints of time, space, and gravity. There are rules on earth that shape our perspective of what is possible and impossible. It is no wonder that when following Jesus, who disregards all of our constraints, we get panicky.

We read the Bible, and we learn in our minds about God's power, it all seems so simple on the page. Then we get into the water of life, and the four-foot deep trials make us question everything. We think God is asking us to do the impossible. This is normal. We don't operate how God does, and we have a choice.

Will we follow and do what seems impossible? Will we be faithful with a small test so that we can experience the wondrous adventure He has planned? Or will we live our lives on the surface? If Peter hadn't started sinking that day, I wonder how far Jesus would have taken him across the water. If we will release our inhibitions and trust Him, I wonder how far God will take us.

Pray

Father, thank you for inviting us to be part of your incredible work. When I feel stuck by my own limitations, remind me that you are limitless. Give me faith to follow you into the impossible so that I can experience all that you have in store. I trust you.

Reflect

In what area of life do I need to trust God with my limitations?

Day Eighty-Eight

Thunderstorms

I love summer thunderstorms in south Louisiana. I am drawn outside just before the skies open and the torrents pour. There is an energy in the air as the gusting wind whips thick tree branches back and forth across the blackening sky. The massive live oaks dance like seaweed in the tide. I stand out in the open, feeling both frightened and strangely alive in the storm's power.

The thunder approaches, sometimes with a deafening clap and other times with a low rumbling that tumbles across the sky. I am small and vulnerable here. I'm unprotected but exhilarated at the thought of being part of something cosmically bigger than myself. Lightning darts down, leaving a scarred pathway to earth.

Through the storm, my Creator humbles me to my proper place of worship and awe. I am not in control. Instead, I let the wind whip my hair, and I embrace the relief of being small.

Read

Listen carefully to the thunder of God's voice as it rolls from his mouth. It rolls across the heavens, and his lightning flashes in every direction. Then comes the roaring of the thunder—the tremendous voice of his majesty. He does not restrain it when he speaks. God's voice is glorious in the thunder. We can't even imagine the greatness of his power. Then everyone stops working so they can watch his power.

Job 37:2-5,7, NIV

Apply

We are born with eternity in our hearts, and we have an internal longing to be part of something bigger than ourselves. Even within Christianity, this often takes the form of doing. We create programs, love others, and serve tirelessly. This hustle for Jesus isn't bad, but it can be distracting.

The details, the worries, and the problem-solving slowly creep in until they take over our attention and energy. The better we manage our duties for Jesus, the more comfortable we become. We check boxes and meet expectations. We view our role as indispensable and our service as irreplaceable. As our dependence on Christ wanes, others' dependence on us increases.

This is a dangerous path. And inevitably, God rolls in a storm to challenge our identity and help us return to a correct relationship with Him. Storms upset the status quo and make us question everything, but they force us to recognize that we are small, and that God is big. The immensity of His power is intimidating but exhilarating. We acknowledge our weakness but breathe in the electric energy of knowing that we have His might flowing through us.

Pray

Father, you are immense and eternal, powerful and incredible. I stand in awe of your majesty, and long to be a part of what you are accomplishing in the world. Allow me to play a role in your plan but to never forget that I am small. Thank you for being in control, so I don't have to be.

Reflect

When was the last time I stood in awe of God's greatness? How does that experience change how I serve God?

Day Eighty-Nine

Going Through the Motions

In the car, my six-year-old asks me to play a song she has learned at church. I put the song on for her and smile as her off-tune voice belts out the words in a way only a mother could love. As I peek in the rear view mirror at her, I notice she is doing hand motions to the song. My breath catches as I realize I had choreographed them myself. *How is she doing my motions?*

Some quick mental math informs me I choreographed the song fourteen years prior. My first job out of college was in children's ministry at a church. My first task was creating moves to the worship songs for the kids. I led this song countless times.

Eight years later, I left the workforce to raise my kids. In those years, I volunteered at my new church to teach song motions to the high school girls who led worship for the kids. And those girls, now in college, are teaching them to my daughter, singing her heart out to the Lord from the back seat. One insignificant task on my to do list fourteen years ago is still bringing God glory!

Read

Before I was born the Lord called me; from my mother's womb he has spoken my name.
He said to me, "You are my servant, Israel, in whom I will display my splendor."
But I said, "I have labored in vain; I have spent my strength for nothing at all. Yet what is due me is in the Lord's hand, and my

reward is with my God." For I am honored in the eyes of the Lord and my God has been my strength.

Isaiah 49:1b, 3-4, 5b, NIV

Apply

The world constantly tells us what is worthy of our time and attention. It sets standards by which we can evaluate success. It tells us to strive, achieve, and conquer. The world has its limitations, and so do we. But God has no limitations. He can feed 5,000 people with five loaves and two fish. He can create everything in existence with a mere word. He can take one minor act and use it to change the course of history.

The accurate measure of success in following Christ is not doing something huge, but faithfully doing each small thing that He sets in front of us. It is making the phone call, showing up with a meal, giving a hug, pouring out a prayer, and extending His love in a million little ways. He doesn't want a grand gesture; He wants a lifetime of obedient steps.

We may never know the impact of our lives, but it is best that way, because creating a personal legacy is not our reward. God Himself, the Lord of Heaven's Armies, the King of Kings and Lord of Lords, beginning and end, is our reward. How sweet it is to be honored in His eyes and to be called His good and faithful servant!

Pray

Father, I am humbled to think about how you have chosen me to display your splendor. Help me to faithfully and obediently follow you in the small things every day, and to find my identity and significance in You as my reward.

Reflect

What seemingly insignificant act of obedience do I need to take pn today?

Day Ninety

That's Not Fair

A common refrain in our house is "that's not fair." My older two girls see everything as a competition. If one does something well, the other will try to do it better, and then announce loudly that they did so. If one has something, the other will demand that they get the same thing. This week we had a special after-school treat. As soon as my daughter finished her brownie, she asked for another one. When the answer was "no," she started pouting.

Knowing how incredibly blessed my children are makes their claims that "it's not fair" especially infuriating. They are so far removed from being in need that they have no context in which to understand how lucky they are. It's true that "it's not fair." It's not fair that they were born into a household with two healthy parents who love the Lord and live in a home with running water, electricity, a full pantry, and clean clothes. In what context is all that they have not enough?

No matter how many times I try to explain how unfair it is that they have so much that others don't, it never helps. They still bicker and fuss and demand what they want. The hole they need to fill is bigger than all the things that they try to stuff into it.

Read

Keep your life free from love of money, and be content with what you have, for he has said, "I will never leave you nor forsake you."
Hebrews 13:5, ESV

Apply

Even though we understand how blessed we are, we still fuss and whine when God blesses someone else in a way that we want to be blessed. How can He keep the desires of our hearts from us if He truly loves us, especially when our desires are good, and we are following Him?

Like kids who crave instant gratification, we forget that all the desires in the world won't fill the hole in our souls. We were created in God's image, with eternity in our hearts. We were built to crave the infinitude of God, who contains the universe. We yearn for the immensity of our Creator, and only He will satisfy. It is interesting in the verses above that the reason for contentment isn't that we get what we want or even that God promises to provide, but that He promises to be there. Our greatest gift is not what God can give us, but God Himself.

God knows that no amount of stuff or blessings will ever keep us content. We will always need more unless we reach for Him alone. Our only satisfaction is in Him! The Creator of everything is with us, each and every moment. He will never leave us or forsake us, and when we tell Him "that's not fair," we forget the blessing that we have in the promise of His presence. In what context could we ever want more?

Pray

Father, it isn't fair that Jesus died on the cross in my place so that I can have your presence. When I want to demand my rights, remind me I have the greatest blessing just by being with you. Help me find satisfaction in your presence rather than searching for fulfillment in anything, anyone, or anyplace else. You are my one true desire.

Reflect

How can I focus on God's presence rather than my desires today?

Day Ninety-One

Changing Seasons

My youngest daughter is two, officially a toddler. Her milestone marks one for me as well. It ends a seven-year season of pregnancy, breastfeeding, babies, and sleepless nights.

I have a long series of distinct seasons in my life, and each feels almost like a different lifetime. I had a college season, a children's ministry season, an inner-city ministry season, and a mother of babies season. Every one of these phases of life has transformed me. As I leave each one behind, it seems like leaving a part of my identity behind, but that isn't true. I am taking a new version of myself into the next season that God calls me to.

Read

Then the LORD said to [Moses], "This is the land I promised on oath to Abraham, Isaac and Jacob when I said, 'I will give it to your descendants.' I have let you see it with your eyes, but you will not cross over into it."
And Moses the servant of the LORD died there in Moab, as the LORD had said. He buried him in Moab, in the valley opposite Beth Peor, but to this day no one knows where his grave is.
Moses was a hundred and twenty years old when he died, yet his eyes were not weak nor his strength gone.
Since then, no prophet has risen in Israel like Moses, whom the LORD knew face to face, who did all those miraculous signs and wonders the LORD sent him to do in Egypt—to Pharaoh and to all his officials and to his whole land. For no one has ever shown

the mighty power or performed the awesome deeds that Moses did in the sight of all Israel.

Deuteronomy 34:4-7, 10-12, NIV

Apply

If there is anyone who understands transitions between distinct seasons of life, it is Moses. For the first forty years, he lives in Pharoah's house, a Hebrew separated from the suffering of his people in slavery. For the next forty years, he is a shepherd in Midian, hiding from his past. For the last forty years, he leads the Israelites through the desert to the Promised Land. At the end of it all, he never steps into his final destination.

Did Moses die with regrets, his goal just out of reach? I don't think so. God Himself buried Moses, and spoke to him face-to-face like a friend. I think Moses' life ended in the best way he could have imagined, in the presence of God, who had walked with him through every moment along the way.

We must hold loosely to what we do and accomplish and cling tightly to the One we follow. Seasons will come and go, each with their varying degrees of influence and impact. What must not change is our dedication to faithfully following God. All the world's success will never compare with knowing God, and at the end of it all, His presence will be our reward forever.

Pray

Father, in each season of my life, help me define success by knowing and following you. Give me the strength to take each step that you place in front of me, always valuing your glory more than the tasks I complete. Thank you for promising to be with me until the very end of the age.

Reflect

How can I grow closer to God in my current season?

Day Ninety-Two

Playing It Safe

My oldest daughter is now riding a horse named Tinka. Tinka has a lot of energy but not much experience. She needs constant direction but is always ready to go! Maya's last horse, Ringo, was old and calm. He has been going in a circle around the ring for so many years that he can't do much else. He is perfect for the beginning rider, but Maya's skills have outgrown his performance.

After a rough lesson with Tinka, Maya told her coach in tears that she wanted to ride a different horse at the show that weekend. Her coach suggested she ride Ringo. Ringo performed exactly as expected: slow, predictable, and half-asleep. Maya earned her first blue ribbon ever and rode well, but the day lacked the excitement of a competition. I would be more proud of Maya coming in last place facing a challenge than winning a blue ribbon while playing it safe. Growth happens when she steps out of her comfort zone.

Read

Do you not know? Have you not heard? The Lord is the everlasting God, the Creator of the ends of the earth. He will not grow tired or weary, and his understanding no one can fathom. He gives strength to the weary and increases the power of the weak. Even youths grow tired and weary, and young men stumble and fall; but those who hope in the Lord will renew their strength. They will soar on wings like eagles; they will run and not grow weary, they will walk and not be faint.

Isaiah 40:28-31, NIV

Apply

How often do we take a risk in our faith? It is easy to get stuck in a rut of safety and predictability in our Christian life. We go to church, read our Bible, and pray before meals. The longer we follow Christ, the easier it is to fall into a monotonous routine. Our view of God shrinks smaller and smaller, and we forget what He is capable of.

We have forgotten who God truly is. God is infinite. In order to know Him and follow Christ, we embark on a journey that never ends. We will never reach the depths of His understanding. We will never exhaust His enthusiasm, love, and goodness. Even in eternity with Him, we will never reach the limit of learning and growing!

In order to know our immense God, we have to step away from the predictable and take risks. We have to follow Him into unknown places that demand more of us than we think we can give. There is no limit to God, and there is no limit to what we can do through Him. He wants to build His Kingdom, but all too often we settle for constructing miniature dollhouses.

If we truly believed that God could do anything, what would we pray for? Where would we go? What would we be willing to risk? And how would the world be radically different? We are ready for the next challenge.

Pray

Father, I am ready to step out in faith. Help me remember that your power and goodness are limitless. Show me any areas in life in which I am playing it safe, and give me the courage to accept a challenge in my faith.

Reflect

In what areas of my relationship with Christ am I playing it safe?

Day Ninety-Three

You've Been Served!

My church had a work day to volunteer for projects, and I decided to bring the girls and teach them about serving. On the way to church, I reviewed with them the importance of having a happy heart and saying yes to whatever job we received.

However, the guy in charge said there wasn't a job kids could help with. On the drive home, I was upset at getting rejected. At home, I noticed my neighbor in the front yard with a plastic bag. Their house had been toilet-papered for Homecoming several days before, and she was evaluating the disaster.

"New plan!" I told the girls. "We are going to pick up toilet paper in the neighbor's yard." I didn't have to say it twice. The girls grabbed our giant trash can, dragged it to her yard and raced around, collecting armfuls of toilet paper. After a few minutes, the neighbor said she had to leave and not to worry about it. But I couldn't drag my girls from that yard until every scrap was gone.

When they had collected an entire trashcan full of toilet paper, they were so excited that they had helped. I had wanted to teach my girls a lesson in service, but instead I got served!

Read

In everything I did, I showed you that by this kind of hard work we must help the weak, remembering the words the Lord Jesus himself said: 'It is more blessed to give than to receive.'

Acts 20:35, NIV

Apply

I learned three important truths about service that day:

1) *We should always look for ways to help others.* I had looked at the toilet-papered lawn for days without thinking of doing anything about it. It wasn't until I was looking for a way to serve that I considered taking action.

2) *We must know our motivations for serving.* Why did the rejection at church bother me? Did I want to be needed? Was I more focused on setting an example for my kids than on actually being helpful? When we serve for any reason other than to bring God glory by loving those that He loves, we may boost our own morale, but we won't find genuine joy.

3) *We must know our expectations when serving.* I have to fight the urge to put a tiny tally mark next to my name, as if my service deserves recognition. The moment we start to keep score, we forget there is nothing of value we could ever accomplish that doesn't come through God's forgiveness and grace.

My daughters found joy in completing a job that no one saw them do, that no one thanked them for, and that had no known reward. I want to be more like them. I'm so glad that they could teach me a lesson in serving.

Pray

Father, open my eyes to the needs of those around me. Help me see how you want me to serve and to follow through with no expectations. Allow my only motivation to be your glory. Thank you for your forgiveness and grace that are given to me with new mercy every morning, as I continue to learn how to follow you.

Reflect

How can I serve someone this week?

Day Ninety-Four

The Horse Tail

As a kid, I loved to play with and used most of my spending money on a collection of small plastic pets that came with accessories. I pulled them out of the attic to share with my daughters. They love them as much as I did but lack the same level of respect for them. To my frustration, they lose and break pieces.

Then Maya cut the tail hair off of the plastic toy horse. She could tell that I was upset at my childhood toy being destroyed. Half an hour later, she came to me with a big smile on her face.

"Mom, you are going to be so happy with what I did!"

I was almost too afraid to ask, "What did you do?"

She pulled the toy horse from behind her back. In the place of the missing tail, she had duct taped some curly black thread to create a new tail. "I found a string in my room and when I pulled it apart, it was curly, and I thought it would be perfect to make a new tail for the one that I ruined! Isn't it great?"

It was great. I don't really care that much about the horse's tail, but I care a lot about my girls' sense of honor and respect. I was so pleased, not by her duct-taped fix, but by her earnest desire to please me.

Read

His pleasure is not in the strength of the horse, nor his delight in the legs of the warrior; the Lord delights in those who fear him, who put their hope in his unfailing love.

Psalm 147: 10-11, NIV

Apply

When Maya fixed the horse's tail, she wasn't doing it to get out of a punishment, from a sense of shame or guilt, or even to earn praise. She was doing it simply because she loved me and wanted to please me. That was the most beautiful gift that she could have offered. Even though the fix was far from perfect, her heart was in it completely.

God wants the same from us. We think of God as a judge who imposes a set of rules. All He wants from us is to do the right thing, to stay in line, and not rock the boat. If we check all the boxes and do nothing wrong, then we will stay on His good side.

The Bible shows us that God is nothing like that at all! God is not a judge but a Father. While He wants us to make wise choices so we can be in a relationship with Him, unhindered by sin and distraction, He doesn't desire our sacrifice but our love. Instead of merely requiring us to follow a set of rules, He wants us to adore Him with our hearts. He wants so much more than obedience; He wants our love and affection.

Pray

Father, I want to please you! When I believe that you just want obedience, remind me of how much you desire my love. Let my service for you come from a burning desire to please you rather than from guilt, shame, or obligation. Thank you for creating me to please you and for being pleased with my heartfelt, yet imperfect, love for you.

Reflect

How can I please God this week?

Day Ninety-Five

An Open Book

I had the best compliment this week. My oldest daughter is six years old and learning to read and write. When I went to wake her up for school in the morning, she was waiting for me with a big smile, eager to show me her latest creation.

She had duct-taped construction paper pages together to make a book. It had a cover, a story, illustrations on every page, and a drawing of herself in the about the author section. She even drew a bar code on the back.

"I don't know what the lines are for, but all the books have them."

She has watched me write, edit, and publish books for her entire life, and this pastime seems normal in our house. Don't all stay-at-home moms write books while their kids nap?

She read the book out loud to me, about a day in the life of her cat. The characters were one-dimensional and the plot painfully straightforward, but I was riveted. I was proud of her creativity, honored at her emulation, and awed by her industrious ingenuity.

Read

Love the Lord your God with all your heart and with all your soul and with all your strength. These commandments that I give you today are to be on your hearts. Impress them on your children. Talk about them when you sit at home and when you walk along the road, when you lie down and when you get up. Tie them as symbols on your hands and bind them on your foreheads. Write them on the doorframes of your houses and on your gates.

Deuteronomy 6:5-9, NIV

Apply

Our lives are an open book. How we spend our time and treasure shows where our values lie. If we love achievement and recognition, we try to climb the ladder and earn praise. If we love and value others, we put the phone down and look them in the eye. If we love attention, we curate our appearance. If we love God, we open our Bible and seek Him first in all things.

Even more, our values influence the people around us, especially our children who are always observing our priorities. Our actions set the tone for what normal life can look like. If our hearts are filled with God's truth, we can't help but engage with the world through a lens of faith. Our beliefs change how we interact with others, how we lead our families, and how we approach our work.

My daughter thinks it is perfectly normal to write books in her spare time because that's what she sees in our house. In the same way, our decision to choose to walk in God's wisdom each day will change the expectations of what life can look like for those around us. The greatest way to share our faith is to first live in it fully ourselves.

Pray

Father, thank you for allowing me to have an influence on those around me. Help me rely on you, so that others will see your character in me. Let me bring hope to a world that is looking for truth.

Reflect

What values am I showing to those around me?

Day Ninety-Six

Kernels of Wisdom

Yesterday I got to use a pair of tweezers to pull two dry corn kernels out of my two-year-old's nose. She had found the corn kernels on the floor of the van leftover from our visit to the corn maze a few weekends ago.

As I was driving down the road, I heard her say in a stuffed up voice, "Mommy, can't breathe. In my nose."

I pulled over in the nearest parking lot and jumped out. She had one large, hard corn kernel shoved in each nostril. One was not in as far as the other, and I was able to get it out with my fingers. She had shoved the other one way up there, and the shape of the kernel matched her nostril exactly. It was like a custom fit nose plug. Thankfully, I could get it out with a pair of tweezers, and she could breathe again.

Read

"If you keep your feet from breaking the Sabbath and from doing as you please on my holy day, if you call the Sabbath a delight and the Lord's holy day honorable, and if you honor it by not going your own way and not doing as you please or speaking idle words, then you will find your joy in the Lord, and I will cause you to ride in triumph on the heights of the land and to feast on the inheritance of your father Jacob." For the mouth of the Lord has spoken.

Isaiah 58:13-14, NIV

Apply

During COVID, we all took a break from activity-filled schedules in a forced season of Sabbath. It was a blessing in disguise to clear out the excess. We realized the parts of our lives necessary for a healthy rhythm and those that weren't. For a long time, many of us kept our rhythms simple, only adding in the life-giving aspects.

As the years roll on, it is easier and easier to slip back into the hustle lifestyle from before the world changed. Instead of shoving things into our schedules because they fit, we need to take the time to evaluate if fitting them in will keep us from breathing.

My toddler thought her nose was a perfect place for a corn kernel, and indeed, it fit just right. However, it restricted the very passage she needs to breathe and survive. Our nose has holes, but they only work properly if we leave them clear.

When God created the world, He designed it with a built-in space for rest one day a week. And this sacred margin only serves us well if we keep it uncluttered. Are we seeking God's face or His approval for our many accomplishments? Let us not fall into the trap of adding in anything "good" at the cost of precious time alone with God. We must give ourselves space to breathe in His peace, comfort, and presence.

Pray

Father, thank you for creating a space and time for us to worship you, rest, and reflect. Help me remember that the Sabbath only blesses me when I use it for its intended purpose. When I am tempted to say "yes" to one more thing, help me discern whether it will draw me closer to you or take away from our time together.

Reflect

What is keeping me from restful time with God?

Day Ninety-Seven

Wash. Rinse. Repeat.

I'm going to pull back the curtain and give you a peek into my writing life and show you where the magic happens. I write from home during early mornings, late nights, and toddler nap times in my home office, which is in the laundry room. The room is 5 x 10 feet and houses the washer, dryer, ironing board, my desk, and a shelf for inventory and shipping supplies. It's pretty cozy.

This set up has done wonders for my laundry routine, because if I want to work, I have to get the laundry done first. The bar for the hanging clothes is above my desk, so I have to put the hanging clothes away in the closets before I can sit down at the computer. And I pile the clean clothes from the dryer onto my desk chair. So before I sit in the chair, I have to fold and put away the laundry.

If I ever feel like I have writer's block or just can't seem to get into a writing rhythm, it usually has nothing to do with the writing. It means I need to do the laundry.

Read

Therefore, if you are offering your gift at the altar and there remember that your brother or sister has something against you, leave your gift there in front of the altar. First go and be reconciled to them; then come and offer your gift.

Matthew 5:23-24, NIV

Apply

We know God is always with us and His presence is everywhere, and yet we go through seasons where He feels distant. This distance isn't caused by God being far away physically, but He may seem to be far away spiritually. There is an unholy attitude blocking His voice or a habit of sin in our lives, keeping us from acknowledging or recognizing His presence, even though He is there, just as before.

We can't move forward until we deal with the spiritual clutter distracting us from God. In the same way that I have to deal with the laundry before focusing on work, we have to deal with unforgiveness, repent of sin, and transform our minds to be like Christ before we can live a life that loves others.

I know it sounds like a lot of work. There is no need to be overwhelmed by the task, though, because even when God seems far away, He is still right there with us, continually drawing us back to Himself. We don't have to conquer these roadblocks alone, even when we feel lonely. If your time with God feels forced or your prayers seem scattered, ask God to point out the "spiritual laundry" that you need to deal with first, and then get ready to work.

Pray

Father, thank you for the promise that you are always with me. I am sorry for how I choose my will and interests over yours. Show me the areas that I need your help to repent and make changes so that I don't miss out on the good work that you have for me.

Reflect

What is keeping me from recognizing God's presence and hearing His voice?

Day Ninety-Eight

The Wish List

On a school field trip, each child got to tell Santa what they wanted for Christmas, and he gave them all a candy cane. My four-year-old middle daughter went first. She knows the truth about Santa, but prefers to believe in him anyway. She asked Santa for a living, breathing unicorn to live in the backyard.

My oldest daughter, at age six, is highly logical, and she knows Santa is just a character at Christmas. When Santa asked her what she wanted, she wished for a candy cane, and he gave her one. She hates candy canes, though, so she threw it away.

When I asked her why she asked for a candy cane, she said, "I saw he was giving out candy canes, so I asked for a candy cane. That way, I knew my wish would come true."

Read

You do not have because you do not ask God.

James 4:2b, NIV

I write these things to you who believe in the name of the Son of God so that you may know that you have eternal life. This is the confidence we have in approaching God: that if we ask anything according to his will, he hears us. And if we know that he hears us—whatever we ask—we know that we have what we asked of him.

1 John 5:13-15, NIV

Apply

Unlike Santa, God doesn't answer our prayers according to our works, whether we have been good this year. There is no obligation on God's part to reward us, and we cannot earn His gifts. We know God is almighty and can do what He wants. He can say no to our prayer requests, so what is the point of prayer?

There are two major factors that affect our prayer life. The first is our level of belief. In order for our prayers to have any effectiveness, we must have faith. It only takes a tiny speck of faith, but faith that God can do what we ask. This is where my six-year-old got stuck. She didn't believe that Santa could give her anything more than she already knew she was getting. While that is true of Santa, it isn't true of God.

The second factor affecting prayer is our motivation. We must want something for the right reasons. This is where my four-year-old got stuck. Even if a unicorn showed up in the backyard, she would be incapable of taking care of it or sharing it with her sisters. The request was purely a selfish desire.

So what is the point of prayer? Aside from bringing us into the presence of God, it helps us analyze our motivations and test our faith. Are we asking for things that are safe because we don't want to be disappointed? Are we asking for things that benefit others or just ourselves? Prayer unveils our hearts.

Pray

Father, thank you for hearing my prayers and answering them. Help me trust in your ability to accomplish anything that I ask, and give me the correct motivation when I present my requests. You are so good!

Reflect

Do my prayers need an increase in faith or a change of motivation?

Day Ninety-Nine

Pulling Carrots

We planted carrot seeds months ago, and after waiting and waiting for them to be ready, we finally pulled them up. Carrots are deceiving because the entire edible part is under the dirt, and you never know what to expect until you pull it up.

My girls took turns choosing a carrot to pull until we harvested the entire crop. They looked at the carrot tops to find the tallest, bushiest leaves and pull that one, hoping to find the biggest carrot underneath. They pulled up carrots of every shape and size, some with forked ends, double roots, and strange knobs and bulges.

The best carrots were the ones we pulled last. Their tops weren't very impressive, and we were expecting something scrawny on the other end, but it surprised us to discover long, thick, dark orange carrots connected to the scraggly leafed tops. With carrots, the visible part of the plant doesn't reflect the health of the root. In fact, the more energy the plant puts into leaf development above ground, the less it puts towards developing the root below.

Read

Your beauty should not come from outward adornment, such as elaborate hairstyles and the wearing of gold jewelry or fine clothes. Rather, it should be that of your inner self, the unfading beauty of a gentle and quiet spirit, which is of great worth in God's sight.

1 Peter 3:3-4, NIV

Apply

As we set goals for ourselves, let's be mindful of a few common mistakes. There are many worthy goals in which we can invest our time and energy, and seeing visible results is always rewarding. However, our growth habit is the same as carrots. The most productive growth that we can do is below the surface.

Instead of seeking social media followers, let's become followers of Christ. Instead of gaining resources, let's be wise stewards of what God has given us. Instead of making our names known in the world, let's make Christ known through our words and actions. Let's love well, be silent, seek forgiveness, and accept discipline with humility. These goals won't make the top ten list of those seeking success in this world, but this world is not our final destination.

While everything that we can see and touch is wasting away, we possess a soul that is eternal. Pouring time and energy into knowing God and growing to be more like Him is an investment that we will carry with us forever and ever. Let's not compare our "carrot tops" to those around us; instead let's reach deep into the soil and put our energy into what truly matters. We may not be much to look at above the ground, but when harvest time comes, it will be obvious where our energy was spent.

Pray

Father, thank you for giving me a soul that will last forever with you in eternity. Renew my mind so that I can focus my time and energy this year investing in cultivating a heart that loves and follows you. You are my highest reward.

Reflect

How can I prioritize spiritual growth in my life?

Day One Hundred

Celebration!

This devotion is different, because we have something BIG to celebrate! This is the one-hundredth devotion! Can you believe that we have been digging deep into God's Word together for one-hundred days? I am so grateful to have you to walk with me on this journey of growing closer to Christ. Knowing that we are not alone as we learn how to follow Christ is a beautiful thing!

Read

Open to me the gates of righteousness, that I may enter through them and give thanks to the Lord. This is the gate of the Lord; the righteous shall enter through it. I thank you that you have answered me and have become my salvation. The stone that the builders rejected has become the cornerstone. This is the Lord's doing; it is marvelous in our eyes. This is the day that the Lord has made; let us rejoice and be glad in it.

Psalm 118: 19-24, ESV

Apply

Today is a big day to celebrate! Why? Is it because one-hundred is a big number? Nope. It's because of what that number represents. That number represents one-hundred days spent opening God's Word, reading it, and asking Him to show us what He wants to say. It is one-hundred days of listening to His still small voice, of creating a quiet moment to turn down the noise of this temporary world and focus on the eternal. It is one-hundred days of knowing that you aren't alone in this pursuit of Christ. We can hold each other accountable and grow together!

The verses above are talking about Christ. The gate that the righteous enter through is Jesus. He is the Cornerstone of our salvation. Because of Him, we can rejoice every day, knowing that He has made a way for us to spend eternity with Him. Psalm 84:11 says, "Better is one day in your courts than a thousand elsewhere." Spending time with the Creator of the Universe is something to cherish, protect, and prioritize. It's difficult to do with the many distractions surrounding us, but here in this space, between these pages, we sit in God's sacred presence together, and that is worth celebrating!

I understand if you aren't ready for this book to end. I feel the same way. That is why I send out weekly email devotions, exactly like the ones in this book, every week. You can sign up to get them for free at **greneauxgardens.com/devotions**

Thank you for being part of this community. Thank you for taking the hand of God, who continually reaches for us. Thank you for staying faithful in the tough seasons. I am so glad that you joined me here, and I pray that we will spend the next one-hundred weeks continuing to grow together!

Pray

Father, thank you for your promise to hear us and draw close to us. Thank you for Jesus, through whom we can enter your presence in worship. Thank you for creating a community of believers to help us as we seek you each day. You are everything worth celebrating!

Reflect

How can I keep growing in God's Word? Is there a friend I need to share these devotions with?

Also by the Author
For Moms

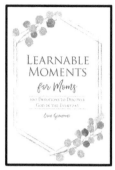

Learnable Moments for Moms: 100 Devotions to Discover God in the Everyday

Inconceivable Redemption: God's Presence in Miscarriage and Infertility (also available in Spanish)

Mary's Treasure: A 24-Day Journey of Reflection, Art, and Poetry

For Kids

The Gold Feather Gardener series

Book 1: The Enchanted Garden (also available in Spanish)

A beautiful gospel allegory for kids ages 4-9.

Book 2: The Quill's Secret

Learn the power of words to build up or destroy.

Escape From Sin's Curse: An Escape Room Card Game

An interactive way to explore the Bible for ages 10 and up.

CPSIA information can be obtained
at www.ICGtesting.com
Printed in the USA
LVHW021208250323
742480LV00008B/396